Ruthless Grieving

The Journey to Acceptance and Beyond

Susan Powers, Ph.D.

MYSTIC MERMAID PUBLISHING

Published by
Mystic Mermaid Publishing
Sag Harbor, New York

Copyright © 2015 Susan Powers, Ph.D.

ISBN: 978-0-69250-843-5

EDITOR: Candace Johnson • www.changeitupediting.com
COVER/INTERIOR DESIGN: Gary A. Rosenberg • www.thebookcouple.com
AUTHOR PHOTO: Kaya Yusi

Printed in the United States of America

Contents

Foreword, vii

Acknowledgments, xiii

Preface, xv

Introduction, 1

PART ONE   Blindsided by Death

CHAPTER 1
Shock and Awe: One Foot on the Ground,
One Foot in the Sky, 10

CHAPTER 2
Rituals: Creatively Honoring the Dead, 39

CHAPTER 3
Warnings: Grieving Can Be Hazardous
to Your Health, 56

CHAPTER 4
Feeling Lost: Giving Yourself Permission, 71

PART TWO   The Emotional Work

CHAPTER 5
Blame and Healthy Anger: Someone to Pin It On, 88

CHAPTER 6
Obsessions: What-Ifs, Regrets, and Resentments, 104

CHAPTER 7
Sadness and Depression: Allowing Your Depth, 121

CHAPTER 8
Grieving the Unheroic Death:
Loss from Addiction or Suicide, 136

CHAPTER 9
Identity, Roles, and Grief:
Beyond Cultural Expectations, 160

PART THREE   Going On Without Them
_____

CHAPTER 10
The Magic of Acceptance:
Nurturing Your Creative Imagination, 180

CHAPTER 11
All That's Left: Tools for Living, 196

CHAPTER 12
Helping Others Grieve: The Art of Presence, 208

Twelve Steps of Grieving, 225

References, 227

About the Author, 231

For Bob and Chris:
All that's left is the love.

Foreword

When Susan's husband, Bob, died, I felt heartbroken for her. Bob was just the kind of guy you'd want to get an extra twenty years with, not twenty too few. The kind of guy you hoped would always be in your life. I felt as if I too had lost someone very wonderful, someone irreplaceable. When three months later she told me that her daughter Chris had overdosed, I couldn't believe it. At once she had lost the person who helped her to feel that she had done something very right in life and the person who made her feel she'd done something very wrong.

I tried to act like a therapist. But the truth is I felt that I had little to give her. Her loss just felt overwhelming, I had not experienced similar such losses, so untimely and unfair feeling. All I could really give her was the stage, my presence, and my understanding of grief theory and the method of psychodrama. The rest was up to her. **Lesson #1: The rest is always up to the client.**

I was grateful that Susan was in my training group and not my client, somehow that made me feel less responsible for her healing. **Lesson #2: We are all responsible for our own healing.**

The thing was, Susan actually took responsibility for her own healing. Holding it with her was one of the heaviest things I have held with someone with whom I have worked. It was so ongoing, so big, and covered two generations. It dipped back into Chris over whom she felt so much guilt, who tied her in such a shameful way to her past. It robbed her of the future she had built with Bob, which was full of so much love, so many friends, recovery, and so much fun.

Susan says that you have to get messy to grieve. I get that, and I guess I can recall many times when Susan's grief looked messy. But truthfully, what lives within me is also scene after scene in which her grief was clean and focused. Susan would come into group knowing what she wanted to work on; she took the stage with a kind of vigor that blew back what was near, like a helicopter landing in a cornfield. What Susan calls "ruthless" grieving seemed to be that she accessed that part of her that was going to reach for life, no matter what, that she was going to find out a way to live out *her* days. With a kind of laser precision, Susan went into her sadness, her shame, her anger, and her pain and blew it around the stage. She wasn't afraid of her tears, and she wasn't afraid to laugh. I think these were equally important. They both ring in my ears, and they were both very beautiful, deep, and rich.

This went on for what felt like years.

Susan had the love in her heart and the ruthlessness in her process both to mourn the daughter she had lost and the one she could never have. Chris was never going to get sober, she was never coming back, she would never be a mother to her two children and a sober daughter to Susan. Bob was gone, his laughter, his winsome and appealing personality, his body, their future together wasn't going to get a chance to be and breathe.

Lesson #3 The person needs to grieve all that was and all that never got a chance to be.

And the shame. That was hard not to rescue Susan from; the truth was that her own addiction and difficult marriage really had influenced her daughter, and to somehow try to white wash that would only slam it down further inside of her. It would be easier but not real. It might make her feel better in the moment but at the expense of self-honesty. Clients, well all of us, need to grieve truthfully and will not be helped by some well-meaning therapist or friend who wants to wrap things up in a neat package. The package was messy, leaky, crinkled, banged up, and goofy shaped.

Lesson #4 Don't back off the pain or the shame. Let it leak all over, it just does.

And Susan had a son. A son who was healthy and making great strides toward a great life. It seemed to me that one of the things that could happen when losing such significant parts of a family might be to psychically kill off the rest, that one could go to either extreme. They might cling too tightly or in their numbness, anesthetize themselves to the experience of the other child, leaving the other child on the sidelines of their pain. If they couldn't have the whole picture, they erased what was left. Susan didn't do that; her son was part of her health, too. Part of reaching toward what was good and strong and there.

Lesson #5 Feel the presence of who is still around.

I often thought of Judith Viorst's book titled *Necessary Losses,* such a good subject. Life is after all full of losses of all kinds, of people, places, and things. But Chris seemed such an unnecessary loss. Bob seemed like he went way too early, he had so much life still in him. But he had lived life. Chris had more or less taken herself out of the game the way that addicts do. To call addiction a death wish is too simplistic. Who knows why someone gets into drugs in this modern world where they are so sanctioned, over-prescribed, and way too available. There are so many reasons, and one of them is simply that at a certain point, a drug begins to have a life of its own, and it lives this life greedily without caring about anything in its path. Drugs and alcohol turn otherwise good people into monsters who seem to care for no one. They rob children of their parents, parents of their children, and lovers of their beloved. These losses appear to be anything but necessary.

So how do you grieve a death that somehow someone brought onto themselves? We don't always feel we have a right to this kind of grief, but it is, in my experience, much worse and a more complicated loss than that of, say, Bob. Bob was a life well lived. How could you say that of Chris's life, Chris who left two little children motherless? Who chose a drug over her little girls, or at least who seemed to. Because we can say that addiction is not a choice, that it's a gene, that it's a disease, and all of these are likely right. But the fact is that it only stops when the addict stops abusing whatever it is they are abusing. So how do you mourn that, all of the anger, the why you's, why me's, and the unresolved, unrequited love? Susan calls it "Grieving the Unheroic Death."

Here Susan has made an important and significant contribution to the grief literature. She has written about these shame-filled, all-too-often hidden, misunderstood, and even more often misnamed deaths. Chris did not die of cancer surrounded by loved ones, saying her good-byes to those she left behind. She died on the side of the road leaving a trail of unfinished business and broken hearts.

Somehow Susan accepted this. No one rushed her process; it took the time it took. But eventually she started coming to group talking about having good days, then many good days, then good days became the norm. She talked about feeling grateful for how full her life was. She looked different and sounded different. She radiated a kind of inner peace and joy. She was strong and supple. Susan found her way back not only toward herself, but toward more of herself, more of life.

Lesson #6 Grieving works; don't quit before the miracle.

Dr. Susan Powers has used her considerable training and knowledge as a psychologist and her experience as one who has "been there" to open up a deep and necessary dialogue on this subject, and I have no doubt that she will be helping people for decades to come as a result.

Lesson # 7 Find what Dr. Powers calls that ruthless part of yourself, hold your nose, and dive into the deep waters of grief that will eventually carry you, on their own natural tides, toward shore, back to terra firma, back to dry land.

One other wonderful feature of Dr. Powers's work with grieving is that she uses psychodrama as well as psychotherapy to heal. To date, I have never seen a method work as well as psychodrama does in resolving grief issues. These concepts and her ability to use this method in helping people to heal their grief are significant contributions not only to the literature, but to the practical approach to helping clients to recover and return to life.

In helping us to mobilize that ruthless part of ourselves that allows us to go on living even when those we love will not, at least they will not live in that particular body as that particular person, Dr. Powers offers hope and healing, a way in and a way out. She takes the reader by the hand and leads them through their own darkness and back into the light.

—Tian Dayton, Ph.D., T.E.P.
Director of the New York Psychodrama Training Institute
author of *Emotional Sobriety* and *Neuropsychodrama*
in the Treatment of Relational Trauma

Acknowledgments

I first want to thank my two geographic communities, which have supported me through the last fourteen years: Sag Harbor, the beautiful and interesting community that is my hometown; and Greenwich Village, all around Perry St., that is my home away from home, where I live and work half the week in New York City. The people in both places have sustained me throughout my journey.

I am eternally grateful to my son, Bill Powers. His care and maturity have carried me through my challenging journey to produce this volume. His suggestion of "Now you need some ruthless editing" is the kind of loving and creative thinking that characterizes his way of being in our relationship.

Then, thank you to my "ruthless" editor, Candace Johnson, my close-in supporter, who has been there in the last three years with her quick, responsive, and intelligent guidance. I appreciate her level of integrity and care. Next, I have to thank my mentor of the last twenty years, Tian Dayton, who led me to Candace and to almost every part of my professional and personal development. Her generous wisdom has been my guide throughout these harrowing and inspiring years.

My friends are my lifeline, and I am blessed with abundance. Creatively and spiritually, I first name Shirley Elias, my colleague and unique pal. She sang Bob to sleep on his last night and harmonizes with my Spirit whenever I reach out to her. Next, my best couple friends, Nancy and James MacDonald, with whom I have the rare experience of a separate and unified alliance in all parts of my journey: from Nancy holding my hand when I heard of the death of my daughter, Chris, to James offering practical help every week with my paper work (and he's also my favorite literary fan). My soulful friend, Anita Wagenvoord, was at my side for the deepest part of my grieving, and for the most confusing and conflicted parts of my writing. Her guidance was priceless and always on target.

I thank Susan Falk, who, in addition to her committed friendship, provided me with an "artist colony" of her own creation in the U.S. Virgin Islands, where I wrote the heart of this book.

I want to acknowledge my entire family who love and support me up close and from afar. My brother, Joe, has been an enormous support in healing from all the family losses. Together we have learned how to enjoy our lives as siblings and as friends. My granddaughters are four people who bring amazing joy to my life, from Kaya and China, Chris's two daughters, now twenty-four and twenty, to Bill's two girls, Kit and Gigi, now sixteen and ten. They are all highly unique and talented females, more than a grandmother could ever wish for. Bill's wife, my beloved daughter-in-law Cynthia Rowley, is an inspiration to me in her example of an authentically creative life. She has loved me through both challenging and exalted times.

I must thank Deepak Chopra and Oprah Winfrey for their contributions to the depth of my spiritual life and to the lives of so many of us around the world.

Finally, I want to thank every one of my friends, colleagues, and mentors, without whom the success of my professional life as a clinical psychologist and psychotherapist and of my personal journey to acceptance and the joy of living could not exist.

Preface

I remember going on a first date with Peter, a very handsome guy, following my prolonged divorce. He was restless and nervous as we waited to be seated at an outdoor cafe on 23rd Street in Manhattan. Then suddenly, he paused and looked up. The moon was full. He stopped talking for a minute and stared at the moon. Afterward, he explained that his mother had taught him to give the full moon some attention and energy. Otherwise, she said, it would work against him and have some bad effect.

I had always loved the moon and followed its phases, but since that evening I've paid more attention when it's full. Although there was no second date, and we each met our future spouses shortly after that, I remember what Peter's mother said, and I try to focus on the moon when it is full. I enjoy the energy it gives me and don't like when it works against me.

On a much deeper level, grief is like a full moon. If we don't give it attention and energy, being conscious of its strength and power, it can affect us in completely unexpected and subtly destructive ways. Grief is not only physical, emotional, and spiritual, but it is also very powerful and ruthless. It can be as ravaging as a serious sickness. In my experience, it must be attended to and respected. If negated, avoided, or denied, grief can create illness and emotional distortions that can result in everything from broken relationships to broken bones. It can cause us to be stuck emotionally in blind alleys of pain and unconsciousness.

We must match the ruthlessness of grief with our own zealous action. Grief does not go away. I discovered, after losing my husband and daughter in 2001, that I had to be proactive and single-minded in my attempts to recover. I had to find a ruthless part of myself in order to prevent the possible physical and emotional damage that could ensue if I became unconscious of my inner process in any way.

In the early stage of grief, one often feels lost. I know I might have remained lost if I hadn't given the process all my attention and creative energy.

As a psychotherapist, I had a lot of tools and insights. But I was feeling lost, and they were of little help to me. However, when I surrendered to all the limitations and distortions that accompany serious loss, I was able to regain my strength and approach the grieving process with courage and even curiosity. I have been able to establish a renewed sense of self and to discover new insights about my life moving forward.

In this book I share with you not only my story, but the tools and actions I used to get through to the other side of grief. You can get through this. You will need to find the fiercest and most creative parts of yourself to come to a renewed sense of self and of your life without your loved one. Whether you are grieving or know someone who is, this book provides a map for the process as well as the support and encouragement to not only get through, but to thrive on your journey.

Introduction

Countless times over the course of a year when I hear of someone who has experienced the death of someone close, I reach out. However, grief is so personal and private that when you are in it, you are often a strange combination of being raw, cracked open, and unreachable—all at the same time. You often wish to take to bed or go far away. I know from my own experience that retreating with a book containing a firsthand account of loss and grieving, with a kind of map for how to proceed, would be very helpful and comforting.

This is that book.

I could say you are about to go on an amazing adventure that will transform you into your deepest, truest self, but you might get angry and quickly close the book. So I won't say that. What I will say is you can get through this. Fourteen years ago, I got through two traumatic losses in a row only by getting a lot of support and using all the tools I had learned in my fifty-eight years of life and sixteen years of a recovery process. I would like to share how I got through and what I have learned about death and life.

Grieving is such a challenging subject that it is painful to write about. Ruthless is my word for it. Grief takes hold of you and doesn't finish until it is complete. I found I had to tap into the ruthless parts of myself in order to push back and push through to the other side of loss. In doing so I was able to surpass most of the destructive aspects of losing loved ones and to become even more whole than I had been before my loss.

In 2001, I lost my husband and daughter within a three-month period. My husband, Bob, died first, of kidney cancer that traveled to his brain. He was sixty-two years old. Two-and-a half-months later, while I was still in the thick of my grief for Bob, my thirty-two-year-old daughter, Chris, died from a heroin overdose.

I write about traumatic grief because my losses were traumatic. All death is not traumatic, but many losses are challenging and bring up other losses and any deficits in our own way of being. Close losses deepen our awareness of the breadth and depth of being human, the vulnerability of the human experience, and the need for full-spectrum living, which is ruthless and compassionate by turn. For me, losing two people I loved was the biggest wake-up call possible to what life is about, what is important, and how to care for myself and others. Loss gave meaning to the spiritual realm, and an entirely new awareness of what some people call "the Other Side."

This is not a religious book, but my losses have deepened my sense of Spirit as well as my awareness of all of the facets of being human. I've had to find the ruthless parts of me to match the ruthlessness and searing pain of losing two people who had been an intimate part of my life.

The weeks and months after loss is a time when you feel like collapsing, doing very little, and there is a place for that, for being gentle and permissive with yourself when you need it. This book is full of permissions needed at each stage of your grief. But overall, as in most challenges in life, we can either use grief to feed our negative beliefs about life and love, about ourselves and our value, to become embittered and more stuck, or we can show up for the challenging phases of loss and find the life lessons embedded in our grief, commit to the pain of being conscious, and change to survive and even thrive in the face of loss.

One aspect of ruthless grieving is being proactive. Even though we often want to collapse and push away the painful feelings, we also need to find that "getting through this no matter what" part of ourselves calls out for help, makes a leap of faith, cancels the lunch with a draining friend, has the coffee with the friend we know we'll cry with. Coming through to the other side of loss is not something that is just a matter of time. As a psychotherapist I have seen that unresolved grief is often at the heart of what blocks so many of us from living productive and satisfying lives. Burying the feelings does not work because they don't go away. They must be dealt with, or they will deal with you.

Another aspect of ruthlessness is doing away with people pleasing. I felt like the social aspects of grieving could kill me. There are some times when I had to "go through the motions" at a required event or a poorly thought-out plan. But I needed to be able to protect myself from other people's needs and wants and the foolish, unhelpful things that well-intentioned people can say. Everything is cancellable, and I cancelled a lot. "That doesn't help me right now" is what I found to say to protect myself from the wounds of other people's lack of attunement to what I needed at any given moment. I found it was my responsibility to protect and care for myself. At the same time, I had to let other people in to help me and sometimes run interference with others. It's a tricky dance, and the prayer for the "wisdom to know the difference" is a great guide. Sometimes we cancel, sometimes we show up, and it's up to us to make those decisions.

You can get through this. I have found many tools and actions that help. The process is messy and sometimes unpredictable, very personal, requiring courage and patience, but doable nonetheless. I know this from my own experience.

Much as I tried to self-soothe in my grief, I found I had to be more proactive about my feelings. I had to take actions. Paradoxically, many of the "actions" were permissions to allow myself all my feelings, including feeling lost much of the time.

The good news is that ruthlessness is not the only attitude that helps; it just sets a tone of self-care and putting yourself first no matter what. The pain comes in waves, but the waves get farther apart with time. In the beginning, pain can feel like one endless tsunami; but that subsides, and the waves become recognizable. Going with the waves is the key. When big waves came at unpredictable times, I learned to let them move through me and to swim the turbulent waters. The important thing is to be conscious, to surrender to what is happening, and to commit yourself to this process. Even if you're not a surfer, you can learn to ride these waves, big and small.

I think I am a good example of conscious and productive grieving. I had access to lots of tools from my many years of psychological work with myself and others, and I used them all.

For more than twenty-five years before Bob and Chris died, I had worked as a clinical psychologist with a private practice in psychotherapy. Grief is a big part of the therapy process, even though it isn't always about losses to death. Avoidance or aborting the grieving process has a profound effect on both individuals and families, and I have helped many clients through that process many years after their losses. It is better to grieve in real time after a loss, but consciously going through the process, whenever you can, is what is needed.

I, myself, had gone through years of therapy to recover from the effects of growing up in my addictive family. My father lost his mother when he was only eleven, and he had clearly never healed that wound. It left him both emotionally shut down and angry. I had to face the ways his emotional state had affected me, and then I had to deal with how his alcoholism had further affected and influenced my life. As a psychotherapist, I knew it was essential that I do my own emotional work in order to be effective in helping others, and I did.

However, after the deaths of two people I loved most in the world, I was lost. I didn't know what to do. I had to surrender to a process that felt very different from the inside. I had helped many clients, but dealing with loss on the inside felt indescribable and disorienting. I had no map, and understanding the five stages of grief was not enough.

In the beginning of his book *Unattended Sorrow: Recovering from Loss and Reviving the Heart,* Steven Levine writes that everyone thinks they are doing it wrong when they are grieving. I thought that, also. Second-guessing yourself is a big part of the process, especially early on. As someone who saw herself as an accomplished woman with a rich, fulfilling life, I was stymied. The grief took my sense of self and shattered it.

Grief will change you. It can tear you apart inside if you let it, but it can also be an opportunity to transform yourself. At first, you are probably an unwilling and even resistant participant. By pushing through that resistance, I have found ways to let grief change me in the direction of becoming more myself than I have ever been. My feelings of grief cut through many of my defenses and the false ways that I had seen myself. They ripped through my codependency and people pleasing in surprising ways that I had not expected. I couldn't do my own emotional work and still do what other people expected of me. At the same time, I began to see life from many different perspectives and to expand my conditioned ways of seeing the world. If my husband and daughter could both die, anything could happen. I experienced a crisis of faith that changed all my perceptions.

Grief does not just go away. Time does not heal all wounds. Grief itself is ruthless. You are facing the realities of death and loss, and it feels like death and loss have won. You need to proactively face the process of getting through loss, and you will come out the other side the victor. It won't bring back the person who has died, but it will lead you into a new life. Despite your loss, you can still be fulfilled and, eventually, even happy.

This book will give you a map for travelling in this unknown territory, the tools to follow your intuitions, the ability to avoid the pitfalls of grieving, and the inspiration to include all your creativity and intuition to travel through to the other side of loss.

It is my experience that you will need a lot of permissions. You will need permission to feel lost and then to find a way to grieve that suits you. I know I did. I needed permission to be a mess sometimes. I needed permission to cry in front of anyone and to allow myself many other uncomfortable actions and inactions. I needed permission not to cry, when others were clearly upset.

This book will give you those permissions and, in addition, it will give you a map for getting through. This loss may be the most challenging event in your life, but it is an event that requires clear and concrete guidance to survive the process, and then to go on to the rest of your life. You will need help, just when you don't want to deal with people or ask for it. Hence this book, which will be a companion and guide through the challenges and self-doubt that are inherent in the process of going through loss. I will share with you the deep compassion I found in myself for what I needed to do and not do and an inner strength that abides with me to this day.

Acceptance is a theme throughout this book. It's important to know you are heading toward acceptance throughout your entire journey of grief—and that begins with accepting your feelings. You cannot do your grief work without accepting that you have and need to express your feelings. That is why the concept of permission is so important.

In the beginning, accepting that someone is gone can feel disloyal; "This I will never accept," can be an attitude that comes up early in loss. I hope to gently lead you through the process toward acceptance—acceptance of everything your loved one was, of how he or she left, of your relationship with each other, and of yourself throughout your grief and beyond to reinvesting in life without that person.

You will always have this loss and will have to deal with it throughout your life. However, the raw, painful, ever-present parts do subside. This book will shine a light on the way through the darkest days toward the light of a creative path, informed by your courageous transformation, into an enriched and fulfilling life. Many parts of grieving are solitary—hence a book. You will not only have to reach out, but you'll have to reach in. And also, if possible, up.

If you're not experiencing grief right now, I'd like to help you understand the process on a deeper level, perhaps to help other people, or yourself, through it when the time comes. If you are in a state of grief, my intention is to share my own experience as a way to help you find and sustain your courage and get you through loss in the healthiest way possible.

HOW TO USE THIS BOOK

I encourage you to pick and choose sections of the book as your interest and needs develop. Of course, you can read it as written, cover-to-cover, but it can be a challenging book to consume. You may not be ready for a lot of words right now. Keep the book close and refer to it often, reading small sections at a time.

I have a few suggestions to help you get started.

At the end of each chapter is a summary called "Things to Remember." Pick a topic and look over the summary for practical suggestions.

Throughout the book I have placed pauses, and I've suggested taking some breaths and considering a few questions. I have placed these pauses throughout the book because grief is not an intellectual process. It is thoughtful and requires intellectual understanding, but it is primarily emotional. The pauses leave room for your emotions and some guidance to sort through them.

I suggest writing down responses to the accompanying questions as well as any thoughts you have as you read through the rest of the text. Get a blank book and make it your grief journal. Having a place to put your thoughts and feelings can be invaluable right now. This writing is for your eyes only and can help you sort out the jumble of feelings and ideas that can feel overwhelming at times in grief.

Everything in this book is optional. There are as many ways to grieve as there are people. Grieving ruthlessly means doing it your way, and it gives permission to find what works for you. Everything is "suggested"—there is no one way to go through this.

For example, if the pauses are significant to you, use them as guides to deepen your emotional process and, if you want, write about them. If you need to skip the pauses on first reading, definitely do so. If you want to read the pauses and not really pause to breathe, do that.

Many people have difficulty with the spiritual aspects I mention in this book. If they make you uncomfortable, just skip over those parts when you encounter them. I have a friend who says he approaches life like a multiple-choice test—if anything looks too hard, he just skips to the next question.

Take what you like and leave the rest.

Remember to be ruthless. Do it your way, starting with how you read this book.

PART ONE

Blindsided by Death

CHAPTER 1

Shock and Awe: One Foot on the Ground, One Foot in the Sky

In 2001, I lost my husband and daughter within a three-month period.

My husband, Bob, died first, of kidney cancer that traveled to his brain. He was sixty-two years old. He was my second husband, and I felt that I had finally gotten it right with a man. Our marriage, like most marriages, was both challenging and fulfilling. We had created a loving, satisfying, and enjoyable life together. We had a strong circle of friends and family, so when he got ill, we reached out to them all and received a great deal of support. Bob was sick for three months. He had a good death, surrounded by people who loved him.

I was bereft.

Two-and-a-half-months later, while I was still in the thick of my grief for Bob, my thirty-two-year-old daughter, Chris, died from a heroin overdose. She had struggled for years with her addiction. Even though I knew she was using dangerous drugs, I thought she would live because Bob had died. I almost thought that Bob's death would save her.

They couldn't both die. But they did.

I was flattened. I just wanted the pain to stop. I tried sleeping a lot, overeating, not eating, not answering the phone, but the pain didn't go away. I had been sober for many years, so drugs and alcohol were not an option.

The term "shock and awe" was used to describe a military strategy in Iraq in the first decade of this century. It caught my attention because the juxtaposition of those two words describes the state I was in right after Bob and Chris died. Early in my grieving, I also had the feeling that I was in a war. Some of the symptoms of post-traumatic stress disorder (PTSD), a diagnosis initiated to describe people returning from war, were also present. There is, in the least, some shock when someone close to you dies.

The contrast of many of your feelings can be quite extreme, and you can feel numb and cracked open at the same time. I felt like I had one foot in the sky and the other on the earth. I needed to be tethered to friends and family, the people I was closest to, in order not to feel like I was floating away. I felt like I was in an altered state, both distant and intense at the same time. The combination of a heightened awareness and a strange unconsciousness made me feel like I had taken the most powerful drug I could imagine, except I hadn't taken anything.

I had looked death in the face, and I did not like what I had seen. At the same time, part of me was peaceful and felt a lot of acceptance. Another part of me was numb, feeling nothing. And then there was the part that felt a giant NO deep within me. I couldn't believe that death is a part of life, but mostly I couldn't accept death.

The states of shock and awe had a very different tone in each of my two major losses. When Bob died, there was comfort and amazement at his peaceful passing. Some of the awe started when he was at home and dying. He was surrounded by people who loved him, and the feeling of peace and otherworldliness in the house was palpable in the last six weeks of his dying process. That was the beginning of a feeling of awe, a wonder and amazement at being present in the moment, a reverence for life, of feeling close to a mysterious process that I had never experienced before. Friends brought over tapes of chanting and we would all join in (something that had never happened in our house before). There were always candles burning, and everyone was quite gentle with each other and with us. I couldn't believe what was happening, and I was amazed and felt very blessed in unexpected ways.

Chris's death was truly traumatic for me and the rest of my family. She was on the other side of the country, and I received a phone call that she had overdosed under a freeway. I felt as though I was trying to navigate a field of landmines that were interspersed with pockets of quicksand. The periods of feeling numb that followed were a welcome relief.

In the Introduction, I explained about traumatic grief and the different levels of trauma that might exist with your particular loss or losses. Mine was traumatic because I lost two of the closest people in my life within a three-month period.

You might take a minute to note how traumatic your loss has felt to you. You also might be numb right now and in some denial about how deeply you have been affected. There is no right answer. Your experience is what is most important throughout your grieving. Your perspective can be distorted, and you might feel mainly disoriented or lost. I believe all loss is somewhat traumatic because you are experiencing death at close range. The disappearance of someone in your life usually affects you in deep and often shocking ways.

Throughout the book I will be asking you to pause, take three breaths, and consider your inner process. This is consistent with my message of ruthless grieving. You will need to face your deepest experience with courage and vigor in order to get through to the other side of grief.

I suggest you pause, take three breaths, and consider: How traumatized do you feel about this loss? How much in shock do you feel? How disoriented or lost? How would you describe what you have been feeling since your loss? What would be a metaphor or analogy of where you have been? It could be helpful to begin writing your thoughts and feelings in a journal—more about that later.

SHOCK

When my husband, Bob, died I felt like I was walking through a dream. Shock is like that. The dreamlike quality had already begun during his illness.

Bob had been sick for three months and died at home. As a result of growing up in my alcoholic family, I had learned to function well in emergencies and what I would call "going through the motions." When my father was drunk, I had to figure out what to do to stay out of the ugly conflict and to help my mother manage the situation. I relied on those same learned skills, using them to make it through Bob's illness and death in a respectful and loving way with the help of friends and family. I also had the support of people from hospice, who were very helpful during Bob's rapid decline. I was not alone, but a deep part of me was pretty numb. The day Bob died is still a little fuzzy to me. That's the shock—it is simultaneously vivid and surreal with flashes of intense emotion mixed with dreamlike images that contain no emotion at all. Of course, these combinations are different for everyone.

My friend Shirley had come to be with us for support at the end of Bob's illness and stayed with us for his last ten days. She helped both Bob and me in sensitive and loving ways. She actually sang to him in the middle of the night when he awoke for medication and continued to sing until he lost consciousness for the last time. I wished I had been the one to do that for him, but I probably couldn't have done it in such a spirited way because of my own pain and sorrow.

Bob's sister also stayed with us for several days before he died.

She sat with him while I tried to get some rest. She woke me up around 5:00 a.m. to say she thought Bob was gone. I got up and saw he was not breathing. I think I cried, but I can hardly remember what happened next. I remember I called the funeral home to come and collect his body. In hindsight, I realize I did that too quickly and could have benefited from more time with him. I was afraid of how I'd feel as his body grew colder. Even though I'd known his death was imminent, having his dead body in the house was frightening.

I remember that I washed Bob's body with help from Shirley and his sister. We had been planning to do that, although I had some fear about it. I knew it would be good for me and give me closure. We let Spunky, our black-and-white cocker spaniel, on the bed during the bathing. Bob had been very attached to Spunky but had been quite oblivious of him toward the end. I had kept Spunky away from Bob for his final week because the dog's unpredictable movements seemed to disturb his rest.

Now, Spunky was up on the bed, sniffing around Bob's nose, looking, I imagined, for his breath and sensing it was not there. I went through the loving motions of touching Bob's body for the last time and getting a favorite sheet to wrap him in. It's difficult to describe the flat affect and the "going through the motions" experience of such an important time. Tears were coming out of my eyes, but I didn't really feel anything.

When the undertaker came, he asked us to sit in the other room while the body was removed from our home. For me, those were the most challenging moments of that morning: sitting on the couch in my home office, crying in my friend's arms, and knowing that Bob's body, wrapped in a sheet, was leaving the house for the last time. At first, I felt pain. Then it passed, and I just felt numb. It felt like my house was not my own, like my body was not, either; nothing was real, and Bob was leaving me. I could not process it all.

Later that day, I drove Shirley to the train. She talked about how well Bob and I had both done that week. I remember telling her on the train platform that I felt complete with my relationship with him. In fact, I said, "I am done with him." I felt shocked when I heard myself say it. I really believed it at that moment, but the process of my internal good-bye to my dear husband had just begun.

I was in this "dream" for at least a week. When I went back to the house, a few friends were there, but it felt like everyone had scattered, like when you walk into a flock of birds on the beach and they all take off. It wasn't true, but I felt totally abandoned. The friends who were there suggested we light a candle and pray. I "went through the motions," agreeing to do it even though I felt disconnected. I remember walking into the bathroom and crying like a baby, and then going back and praying some more.

With the news of Chris's death far away, my reactions were different, and I had more immediate emotion. It felt sudden and unbelievable. Less than three months had passed since Bob's death, and that experience had been so different. Most of the shock of Bob's death had subsided, but the waves of grief and pain were still very present. I was processing my anger and regrets and very much in the center of my emotional turmoil.

My original shock and denial over my daughter's death took the form of not dealing with the emergency collect message from San Diego that I had received from Chris's boyfriend. I had never heard of such a thing. An operator was on my message machine, telling me I had a collect message and to call this number. The boyfriend's recorded voice sounded panicked, saying Chris had overdosed and he didn't know what to do next. That voicemail, which I received first thing in the morning, had come in during the night, and I had no way to call him back. When I didn't hear from him again, I thought she must be all right. I knew that she had overdosed before and survived, and my denial was strong.

I was in that state for twenty-four hours. The next morning I was with my friend Nancy, who was more uncomfortable than I was with that collect message. She suggested that I call the San Diego morgue, and we walked back to my house to call. She held my hand as I got the number and dialed.

"Do you have the body of Christina Powers?" I asked. "Please hold" was the response, and some minutes passed. I remember Nancy's two hands around mine as we waited in my little office on Greenwich Street.

"Yes, we have the body." I wailed, and Nancy held me.

There is a movie titled *Dead Man Walking* in which Susan Sarandon plays a nun helping a convict (played by Sean Penn) through his final days on death row. She tells him, "I will be the face of love as you are dying." Nancy was the hands of love for me, as my whole life changed in that moment.

In shock, I said, "There must be a mistake! Where was she found, what happened?" I don't even remember all the questions I asked.

"I don't know ma'am, but we have the body."

I screamed into the phone, feeling anger like I'd never experienced before. I immediately directed my anger at her boyfriend, enraged that he had not called back. I also immediately felt rage at my ex-husband, a way, I realize now, of getting away from my own feelings of guilt and remorse. Actually, I was mostly angry with myself for what felt like failing her throughout her entire life, especially during my divorce from her father and during my own struggle with addiction. The shock of everything flashed in front of me, as if I was dying.

Now, the worst had happened, and I had to deal with the beginnings of grief all over again. I could not be alone, and friends even came and stayed overnight with me, sleeping in my bed, until after the funeral. Chris's two little girls, who lived with other family members, stayed with me from the day we learned of their mother's death, and we spent a lot of time comforting each other. We immediately looked through many photos and cried. It felt like those photos saved the three of us. The shock and comfort of those early experiences was enormous.

Post-Traumatic Stress Disorder

In the beginning, you are apt to feel numb except for waves of intense emotion that come and go. Although initially a designation for the trauma suffered by war veterans, post-traumatic stress disorder (PTSD) has been used to describe the effects of many other kinds of trauma. The symptoms vary in intensity according to the level of trauma and each person's varying reaction to his or her own emotions. In general, the symptoms of shock are numbness, disorientation and imbalance, confusion, forgetfulness, changes in appetite, sleep disturbance, exhaustion, and hypersensitivity. There is a dazed quality, as if everything is surreal. With severe PTSD, there is extreme hypervigilance bordering on paranoia, dissociation, and nightmares. These are more rare in the grief process but can be present.

The physical functions of the body are often profoundly affected—sleep, appetite, physical balance, and energy level are all vulnerable to this stress. Symptoms vary from person to person, but severe or sudden loss often deeply affects the body. The symptoms feel endless and pervasive, but whatever your experience, you need to remember that you will not always feel the way you do in your early grief.

Surviving the Early Days After Loss

The physical symptoms of shock vary widely, but appetite and sleep are often affected. You may experience loss of appetite. Be sure to make some effort to nourish your body. Your food choices could also be unusual for a while, but eat something, even when you don't really want to. I have a friend who went to bed with pints of Häagen-Dazs ice cream for at least a week when her husband died.

It's also nice to be fed. Let people feed you. They will want to, and you will need the nurturing. The proverbial "casseroles at the door" definitely have a place in early grief. My friend Anita still remembers the turkey that neighbors cooked and brought to her family's house after her sister died suddenly in a car crash. You may have a friend who is good at nurturing and babying you, and you might want them around for a while—until you don't.

Grief is very physical. People who work with the body believe that grief affects the lungs and breathing more than any other part of the body. It is helpful to your grieving process to begin to be more aware of your breathing. Just take a few full breaths right now and notice what that feels like. I will be suggesting conscious breathing to you throughout this book, which may just help your body find some balance and rest.

Grief is exhausting. I remember that I slept unusually long amounts of time after I lost Bob and even more after Chris died. Both times, in the deepest part of shock I was running on adrenaline for about a week, walking through my intense dream, planning the funerals, and I was surrounded by friends and family . . . and then after it was over, I crashed in exhaustion.

Let yourself rest as much as possible. You might not realize how tired you truly are. One symptom of shock is not being able to think clearly. Other common symptoms are forgetting and losing things. Get in the habit of resting frequently and for long periods. Sleep is extremely healing at this time. And being more careful about yourself and your activity is essential.

I remember feeling very off balance and even falling down a few times right after Bob died. I was walking through a parking lot with a close friend of his who had come from Tennessee for the funeral, and suddenly I was on the ground, luckily not hurt. This is all part of babying yourself. Move a little slower and be a little more careful physically. Your physical abilities will return, but they may not be very available at present, especially when you're lacking adequate sleep.

This is also a place, early on, for a tranquilizer or a drink, if you can safely use them. If you are not an addictive personality, a chemical to help the body relax can ease the emergency mode that you may be experiencing. If you need to see a doctor to get some sleeping medication, this is the time to do it for some temporary relief. Just be careful about altering your consciousness too much. It's already altered. As painful as grieving is, you need to go through this, and don't go to someone who will push a lot of pills on you. We'll address this later in the chapter on warnings, but for now do what you need to get to sleep and rest.

Lying down with a book is good if you're able to read. Keeping a book nearby to pick up during a sleepless night can help. Some people can't read for a while, and that's okay. Just a paragraph or two of a favorite book can help you feel less alone. If you can and want to read, get simple, familiar books. If you have a favorite spiritual book, or a favorite of any kind, read a little bit of it, even just a few paragraphs, each day. Poetry or a daily meditation book can also be helpful. Whatever you choose to read, keep books that speak to you close by, and focus on words that can give you the feeling that "I am here—you are not alone."

Be aware that your judgment might be off, and I suggest you don't make any major changes in the first year after loss. Also, the usual filter you use for deciding what to express and what to keep to yourself might be off balance. I mentioned earlier that I blurted out, "I'm done with him," after my husband died.

Permissions

From Day One, you need to give yourself permission to grieve ruthlessly. Saying what you need to say in an open and unfiltered way is one of the early aspects of ruthless grieving. When I was in shock, I discovered the phrase *That doesn't help me right now,* and I needed it. Giving myself permission to do what I needed to do and expressing what I needed to express, no matter what other people thought, was essential for me to get through the early days of loss.

For example, a few days after Chris died, I went with a friend to get enlargements of photographs of her at different stages of her life to show at the wake and funeral. I remember having a strong need to tell the man behind the counter that she was my daughter and had died two days ago, and I did. The friend who was with me rolled her eyes, as if I had done something wrong, but I didn't really care. My judgment was questionable but it didn't matter. You can be ruthless about what you express right now. All bets are off. (I actually wanted to go screaming down the street announcing her death, but I didn't follow that particular urge.)

There is a fine line between checking in with other people about decisions and making intuitive choices. Possibilities were flooding my mind, and I would check in with my friends Nancy and Shirley about some of them. I remember asking, "What do you think about me taking the girls away on a vacation for a week right after the funeral?" and hearing Nancy reply, "Probably not a good idea; you need your adult support right now." In thinking back on this example, I realize the decision was a judgment call, and although disappointed by her advice, I knew I needed other people's guidance or I would be making bad choices. On the other hand, I also remember saying, "I want to have a singer/songwriter friend of Bob's sing a few songs at the funeral home for Chris before we close the casket," and this time, Shirley said, "Go for it." There are no easy answers, but for me, this was an example of allowing my intuition and creativity to guide me. Through the veil of my shock, it felt satisfying. "Do the next right thing," taking the immediate action that is in front of you and not looking too far ahead, is a guiding principle for times like these.

While your friends' advice can be important during this period of impaired judgment, be aware of the need to protect yourself from people during your initial shock. Be aware of expectations. For example, concerned friends might begin to exert pressure for you to be okay or cry more or get organized quickly, none of which might happen for a long while. These expectations might be an ongoing issue in your ability to process your loss, so we will be addressing them throughout the book. In my experience, you can't "people please" and grieve in a healthy way. You can be ruthless on your own behalf, doing one thing at a time or nothing at all, if that is your wish.

Surround yourself with people who loved the person you have lost if you can. That is, if you are up to seeing people at all. If not, choose one person you trust, and slowly introduce others into your environment, as you are ready. You still need to be able to protect yourself from people, at times, and that will continue throughout your grieving. My "That doesn't help me right now" was so useful in many different situations. If speaking that way feels too difficult, find ways to remove yourself from a situation or conversation by saying something like, "Excuse me, I have to . . ."

Sartre wrote "Hell is other people," and you might be experiencing that right now. People might not know how to relate to you at this time, nor you to them. I felt alienated and not able to relate to people's everyday situations for a while, even feeling resentful at times when some people would try to connect to me in my grief. Hearing statements like, "I felt like this when my mother died ten years ago (tears)" taught me to ruthlessly protect myself by thinking and sometimes even saying, "I can't take care of your needs right now."

You know the difference between people who are relating to you and there for you with a story, and people who need to have their own platform and do nothing but drain your energy. Stay away from the latter. Sometimes Sartre was right. In intense grief, other people can feel hellish and even dangerous.

Give yourself permission to cry in front of anyone at any time. I have a theory that one reason people can get so isolated when they have lost someone close is because they refuse to cry in front of other people (or are afraid to) and so stay alone. Maybe I've heard "I hate to cry in front of anyone" a little more often because of my work as a therapist, but I think you might recognize that a lot of people feel that way. Don't buy in. Cry your heart out if you need to. You've had a major loss, and tears are completely natural. Don't stuff them down, and you don't have to apologize for crying or expressing deep emotion. I remember crying really hard as I talked with a good friend on the telephone and saying through my tears, "And I was doing so well." I'll never forget her response: "You're doing so well right now."

Pause. Take Three Breaths. Consider: How much "people pleasing" do you generally do in your life? How capable have you been at asserting yourself in general, or getting people to back off when you need to? Could you tell someone, "That doesn't help me right now"? I encourage you to try it. You have a new energy and power from this loss. Use it when you can.

You need lots of permission to have feelings at any time and to express them. Remember, your feelings of grief come in waves. I call it "surfing your emotions." "Uh oh, here comes another wave." You get used to it.

Emotions move. There is motion in emotion. Let your emotions move through you. Cry, laugh, rage—whatever you need. I was recently at the funeral of three little girls who died in a fire in Connecticut. Their mother bravely gave the eulogy through her tears. She spoke of how her three little girls had embodied love and asked everyone there to take her girls into their hearts and express love more freely in their honor. It was amazingly sad and beautiful at the same time. When it was over, she walked down the aisle of the church on her ex-husband's arm, wailing. Some people have called it full-spectrum grief—I call it ruthless in the best sense of that word.

Pause. Take Three Breaths. Consider: What are some ways that you need to give yourself permission right now? Perhaps you need permission to be alone, permission to need other people and not be alone? Permission to cry or not cry, permission to be how you are right now? Permission to breathe and just exist? Consider writing some of these in a journal.

Ruthless grieving allows you to feel more freedom throughout the process. You need this early on to navigate the social aspects of people gathering around you and dealing with traditional events (like funerals, wakes, or sitting shiva) when you are in early shock. One rule of thumb is to refrain from major changes in the first year, but that doesn't mean you will. When Bob died, it was February, and I decided to rent out my house and go traveling for the summer. It seemed like a good idea. I had a strong desire to change a lot all at once. But that plan changed and became impossible when Chris died that April. Then I clearly needed my home and to stay put.

Ruthless grieving lets you make some unusual decisions. Do whatever you feel your intuition is guiding you to do. Don't give away all your money and move to India, but short of that, let yourself be guided. This could be a good time to consider doing some of the things you always dreamed of, but don't execute the plan this week. Over time, you will develop a sense of a new future. Let yourself have fantasies, but don't try to fulfill them right away. This flooding of new ideas or old wishes is part of the awe of a close loss. Your mind and heart are changing, and I suggest you just let them.

After Bob and Chris died, my brother bought the boat he had always wanted and the piano of his dreams. However, I think he might still be paying them off. There is a fine line between spontaneity and intuition and poor judgment and impulsivity. Grieving can give you the opportunity to be more yourself and change the way you live your life, but take your time and check in with others whom you trust. We will address these deeper issues in the last two sections of this book.

Right now, you may not be able to get out of bed, so those ideas may seem like a pipe dream. Mostly they are for now, but let yourself dream as the ideas come to you. There can be a lot of inspiration right now. Eventually, you will get out of bed and you'll know when you're ready.

The way I felt (and didn't feel) after my husband and daughter died reminded me of a custom I had heard of in a Native American tribe in the West. The person who had lost a loved one would sit and rest in a deep hole dug in the earth. People would pass down food and water until the mourner was ready to emerge. I could relate to that kind of need. You can create your own version of sitting in that hole in the earth in whatever way possible. A well-known treatment for PTSD is the reduction of external stimulation. Your hypersensitivity at this time might demand this approach. Lots of people take to bed for a while or don't leave the house. I got a lot of solace from just imagining that hole in the earth and imagining sitting in it for as long as I needed.

I do believe that permission is key right now. Losing concern for how it looks or what people will think about what you are doing will help. For the time being, strike the word *should* from your vocabulary.

I have always had a tendency to overextend myself, so pacing myself has always been important. When I was grieving, that was essential. Remember, grief can be exhausting, so resting and pacing yourself is more important than usual. A friend of mine who recently lost her husband told me that as long as she is busy, she is fine, but when she stops, the feelings hit her. She busies herself with doing one or two things, like writing thank-you notes for people's condolences or sorting out just a few of her husband's things, and then she collapses. Give yourself permission to find your own pace, and trust it, even early on. Your body will tell you what you need, and so will your intuition.

AWE

The experience of awe after someone close to you has died is difficult to describe. It comes and goes, interspersed with being in shock, or feeling numb or overwhelmed. It is part of grief, and I want you to know it is not unusual to have moments of inspiration and even bliss in the middle of deep pain or numbness.

Awe is the experience of amazement at life and being alive. You might feel a sense of wonder, or a deep reverence for life. It is a sense of otherworldliness. It's not always present in grief, but it often is.

You get glimpses of your truest, deepest self at the strangest times. Be available to notice and even appreciate them. I experienced awe a lot when Bob was dying, and it continued after he left. It can be part of being cracked open by the shock of a death close to you. It can also feel confusing: "How could I be feeling so open and powerful when someone so close to me has died?" It often happens in moments amid pain or shock. Be available for it, and let yourself take it in.

Although these experiences can happen anywhere, be sure to surround yourself with nature sometimes, even though you might not want to go outside at all. Nature can be a great source of awe at any time and can be particularly nurturing and helpful in grief. I think that is why we have so many flowers around funerals and burials. Bring flowers in, if you're not going out much. *Awe-inspiring* is a description of many different experiences, and I encourage you to be open to these when you least expect them.

A sunrise or a sunset can have special importance at times like this. I still remember sitting by the Hudson River on the evening of 9/11, seeing and smelling the smoke from downtown, watching the sun go down over New Jersey, thinking about Bob and Chris having died a few months before, and knowing the world would never be the same.

If someone has been ill and suffering with pain, there is often relief and even joy at his or her passing. Of course, there is also pain and sorrow, but relief is often some part of dealing with a death from illness. And with it can come a kind of awe. Moreover, at any death, the release of energy and a sense of someone we have loved being lifted from "this veil of tears," even just from the human condition, can create a sense of awe.

The sense of awe was palpable in the room when Bob was dying, and I felt a lot of awe when he was gone. It is a sense of otherworldliness and profound peace. When loved ones die, there can be an experience of wonder at their disappearance; where have they gone?

One of the amazing things about waves of grief is that often in between the waves you feel okay and even a little amazed. I remember picking up my littlest granddaughter, China, then six, right after we found out her mother had died. She sat in the backseat of my Honda and said, "I'll never laugh again." I told her she would, and I pointed it out when, a few minutes later, we smiled about someone we saw on the street in an odd outfit. Life goes on—amazing.

The kind of amazement and awe you might experience can be confusing and inspiring as well. Sometimes you might feel like you are losing your mind or going crazy. You most likely are not. Awe can give you a kind of creativity and attunement with other people and with nature that can feel new and otherworldly. Throughout this book I will be encouraging you to stay aware and to call upon your open, creative spirit to help you survive and persevere in dealing with your loss.

Permission to Be Alive

Survivor guilt is a part of loss and can be a giant block to grieving. I felt it with both losses, but because I worked on it after losing Bob, I knew more what to do when Chris died. I needed permission to be living when they were dead. There was a pull to go with them, and I felt like death myself for some days.

A few days after Bob had died, I went to have a session with the healer who had helped Bob and me when he was dying. I felt worse than I could ever remember feeling. She had helped me communicate honestly with Bob, as we became aware that his condition was terminal. I remember her sitting with both of us about a month before Bob left, and her helping me to tell Bob that I accepted if he had to go, but I preferred he stay with me and live on. I guess she helped me to give Bob permission to die.

But now, after he'd departed, I needed a different kind of permission. It came to me as soon as I lay down on her treatment table. I remember how surprised I felt. "I need permission to be alive," I said. I also realized at the same time that neither she, nor anyone else, could give me that permission—I had to give it to myself.

I lay on Susan Grey's table and told myself it was okay I was alive. I cried and cried and felt my own energy coursing through my body. I had to affirm my life apart from Bob. It was a pivotal moment in my grieving. I found I needed to repeat that permission often, to be "on my own side" in my grief and sorrow. In general, I practiced it daily, and it helped me. "I am willing to be alive today," I would say, or sometimes, "I accept that I am alive as me right now."

Pause. Take Three Breaths. Consider: Have you experienced survivor guilt? It can be subtle, but it is a feeling of not having a right to be alive accompanied by an internal deadness. Just give yourself permission to exist in your body right now as yourself. Remember, you are the only one who can give that permission. Take a few more breaths. Look around and see that it has to be okay that you are alive right now.

We will be exploring and deepening that permission to be alive throughout the book. There are different levels of that permission. For right now, you just need to be able to breathe and feel your life force in your body as you. Know it is natural to experience a pull to go with your loved one. Resist that pull and breathe.

The Other Side

When Bob died, I felt like I had a spiritual "in." There was no way that I wouldn't communicate with him—he was my closest friend and ally. Where was he? I looked in the clouds and imagined he was there. I slept with his shirt and even wore it. Everything was different and I couldn't understand much of anything at times.

I tried meditating to make contact with him, but all I had was noise in my head, mostly questions. Where did he go? Why would he leave me? Is there an afterlife? For me, the answer to that one was a clear *yes*. But what is it like for him? Could he see me?

Many people look for signs, and that helps them. I looked for signs of Bob and of Chris, and sometimes they came to me. More often, they came unbidden when I wasn't looking at all. With Bob, the sign was mostly a warm feeling. Once when Chris was still alive, I asked Bob, who had just passed, to help Chris. This was part of my "in" feeling about Bob being on the Other Side, and I felt him say, "Okay, okay," like he was saying "Stop nagging me."

For the first months after her death I would occasionally hear Chris's laugh in my head. At first, it was startling and a little scary. Then it became a comfort and, for me, a sign that she was safe and even joyful.

Many signs are more specific. During the month after her partner passed, my friend Susan saw his profile in a cloud outside her window. It included his beard and glasses, and, I think, little wings.

These signs often appear from nature. They are comforting, creative, and who is to say they aren't real? At the funeral of a young woman in her twenties who died suddenly, a bird flew into the church and stayed during the whole ceremony, hovering over the casket. The girl's family was convinced that the bird was the presence of her soul and proof that she lived on. Another family I know lost their youngest son, whose nickname was Bug. After he died, they always noticed bugs when they were together and were convinced that he was visiting. My friend Shirley was in my backyard shortly after her husband died when a butterfly landed on her arm. It lingered with her for a very long time. She decided it was her husband visiting.

When Bob was dying, I read the *Tibetan Book of Living and Dying*. What I got from it the most was the suggestion of telling (mostly internally) the person dying or who has died to "go to the light." It's quite a mystical phrase. I tried it, and it gave me a lot of comfort while he was dying and after he was gone. I had the idea of helping him travel to the Other Side, and the concept of Light made it appealing and acceptable. It also gave me a feeling of light for myself, in and around me.

One of the most awe-inspiring moments in my grief occurred at Chris's wake. My ex-husband was a Catholic and believed in having a traditional funeral and a wake two days before. I was in shock and had no alternative to suggest. I did not want an open casket but had no strength to oppose it. My son Bill and I decided to let my ex-husband arrange the whole event. There is a place for established rituals, especially when there is no way you can create your own on the spot. (We will address the whole spectrum of choices around rituals in the next chapter.)

It was early spring, and when I arrived at the funeral home I was struck by the sight of a weeping cherry tree in bloom at the entrance. I paused and felt amazed and inspired by its beauty. But moments later, I was shaken and frightened when I went up to see Chris's body for the first time. What I saw was that she was gone and, at the same time, in total peace. The words in my head were that she had gotten the same peace Bob had. What was left was this three-dimensional photo of her being. I saw the beauty of who she had been and had a firm knowledge she was okay and at peace. I am eternally grateful to my former husband for arranging that wake and for the early healing I experienced in that funeral home. It was an otherworldly feeling and a deep inner knowing at the same time. I felt my deep love for her and awe at the miracle of her life and her death, all at the same time.

My awareness of myself and other people changed early in my grieving. I remember looking at people, especially couples, or mothers with their grown daughters, and thinking, "How did they both stay alive?" I was also so aware of being alive and how alive other people were. I experienced the awe of being alive and seeing the life force in others' bodies, in contrast to seeing the dead bodies of close loved ones.

After Bob's death I noticed couples everywhere and felt envious at first. The envy and pure pain was even stronger after Chris died. I was painfully aware of all my friends with grown children (especially daughters) who were living their lives, and I was focused on how much they took for granted having them alive. It was painful to hear stories about their grown kids (especially daughters) and sometimes I had to tell them that their stories were too much for me at any given moment. On the other hand, I was amazed that life goes on and that people had what I had just lost.

Nature, in general, also offered me a different awareness. There is really something to having all those flowers around at a funeral. Those flowers looked more beautiful than I had ever thought they were. I kept them close to me, and I felt their presence until they also were dead.

There is something profound about emotional pain that brings some people to awe. I have heard people speak about the pain/joy connection, which is beyond understanding. There have been exceptional moments in my life (some people would call them spiritual awakenings) when I experienced myself laughing and crying at the same time. The first I remember happened at the ocean after I returned from taking Chris to her first rehab in Minnesota. She was sixteen, and I had been crazed with fear that she would die of her addiction. It turned out that a bed was ready in this busy hospital for adolescents at the same time that she was ready to surrender and go for treatment. After flying home from Minnesota, I stood on the beach on that spring day and laughed and cried that she was safe, and my thought was that the universe had known all along that she would survive. I felt the universe "knew" everything and I didn't need to worry about anything ever again. Of course, I have, but that moment was the beginning of a deeper awareness of spirituality.

Spirituality and Awareness

Throughout the book I will be referring to my spiritual life. I want you to know that this is in the broadest sense of the word. The entry into a sense of Spirit is wide and deep. For me, appreciation of the beach or a sunset is as spiritual as a church ceremony is for someone religious. There is a place for all of it, and there are as many spiritual paths as there are people, in my opinion. It's a wide hoop into the spiritual realm, and I believe everyone has it in them.

Don't be surprised at the internal roller coaster and the unusual twists and turns your feelings may take in grief. If you are reading this book, you are alive right now. Take a moment to attempt to appreciate that fact—give yourself permission and the acceptance of being alive in this moment. Doing that is one of the most spiritual practices I know.

When we are cracked open, which we often are in early loss, we can feel pain and a sense of wonder and amazement at the same time. In grieving, our sense of the spiritual dimension changes. Some people start to have a strong sense of "the Other Side" more than they ever had before. We want to believe in that, maybe need to, and those kinds of experiences often present themselves after the death of a loved one.

I interpreted many of my experiences during Bob's illness and death, and with Chris's death, as spiritual, and they intensified my belief in that dimension. I mentioned previously what happened for me at Chris's wake and funeral, but many experiences occurred with Bob both before and after his death.

I already had a strong sense of what I call Spirit before Bob was diagnosed with kidney cancer. I had learned to pray and meditate over the course of my own therapy and recovery process.

I had been Catholic until I left the church in the late 70s. I left during the time of "God is Dead," when everyone was questioning everything. I related to the questions, but had no answers. I had been traumatized as a child by a lot of teachings about "burning in hell for eternity" if you did something bad, or even if you thought about it. I once had a writing exercise in which I was asked to characterize my childhood. I wrote, "I grew up in Queens, New York, in the Middle Ages."

My family history was filled with addiction, joy, and pain. My father was an active alcoholic until I was thirteen. Because of this history and related problems in my first marriage, I started going to Al-Anon, where friends and family members of problem drinkers share their experiences and learn that they are not alone in the problems they face. There, I heard people speak about all different relationship problems and the idea of a Higher Power or the energy of the universe helping them. I heard, "You need a new Higher Power if you feel punished or judged by yours." In those Al-Anon rooms in Westchester, I was able to sense a different relationship with the spiritual realm. It was the group that first gave me a sense of Spirit. The phrase "where two or more are gathered" developed a deeper meaning for me at that time.

I can't tell you how many people I have asked to "tell me about your spiritual life," who think I am asking about their religion. So often their response is about how long ago they stopped going to church, or "I'm not religious." I find that very sad, not because of an investment in people believing in God or religion, but because I know there is a spiritual dimension that gives meaning and comfort to many people when they broaden their perspective of Spirit and find ways to connect to it.

The spiritual sense in the room when Bob was dying was palpa-

Shock and Awe: One Foot on the Ground, One Foot in the Sky

ble. We had put the hospital bed in our dining room next to the fish tank. Watching the fish swimming around was meaningful to us both. We had loved going to the tropics in winter and snorkeling with tropical fish in the warm, sunny waters of the Caribbean. We'd also had a seasonal ritual of bringing the fish into the fish tank from the little man-made pond in front of our house each winter. Those fish were a presence in the room during Bob's decline. He would be gone when the time came to put them out into the pond again in the spring.

Bob and I both developed a sense that he was leaving and that he was going somewhere. It was so clear, and yet mysterious at the same time. John Edwards, a spiritual psychic, had a daytime TV show we wound up watching together during Bob's last six weeks at home. John Edwards told people about the Other Side (which was also the name of his show). We would watch it and try to figure out what cues people were giving off that gave him this amazingly accurate information about dead relatives. After playing with this idea of the Other Side and laughing some about how bizarre it seemed, we decided Edwards was the real deal, and I think it comforted us both.

It became clearer and clearer to us as time passed that Bob was going to a spiritual place. For instance, he had a niece who visited and, unbeknownst to us, was only a few weeks pregnant. Bob had a dream about her baby, and after telling her about it, she then admitted she was pregnant. It became clear to both of us that Bob was going to where that baby was coming from. We were living a mystery every day, and we felt the awe associated with that mystery in those six weeks before Bob left.

I recently heard a story from a friend of her mother's death. Her mother always told her, "If you are going somewhere, put on some lipstick," and she practiced what she preached. When she was at the end of her life she stopped putting on lipstick, but the day she died, she asked for her lipstick and put it on. The whole family was

33

amazed at her knowing and her intuitive preparation for her own final journey.

We all maintain our denial, when we need it, until we are able to let it go and face what is happening. Bob resisted the deepest sense that he was dying until about two weeks before his actual death. The pain in his bones from the metastasized kidney cancer was mounting, despite the pain medication administered by the hospice nurses. One day he decided he was ready to go.

Years before I met Bob, I had heard Elisabeth Kübler-Ross speak at Riverside Church in New York City. Her message was about facing the reality of death as a part of life. I cried when she spoke about how she valued dying consciously and how she supported and grew the hospice movement to help people leave their bodies with some awareness. The experience of her talk helped me begin to accept that death is a part of life and I wanted to be as conscious as I could when I died. I also learned that day how important it is for loved ones to be willing to let the dying person go.

About a week and a half before Bob's death, he began crying about dying and about us never being together again. After we cried together some and held each other, I repeated to him, "I accept if you have to leave, but I prefer you to stay." Sometimes it's a fine line between accepting that someone is dying or has died and a feeling of rejecting that person. There is often some relief right after a loved one dies, and it's important to know that the relief is a natural part of the process. It does not signal something negative in the relationship. A lot of our talks were about how much I valued and loved Bob, and he expressed the same to me. Then we would hold each other and cry some more.

Bob was still at home, next to the fish, when he finally went into a coma. We all thought that was it, but after about twenty-four hours, he woke up, told me he loved me, and asked to have his diaper removed. Then he fell back into a coma and was dead within a few hours. (That was when Shirley sang him to sleep that last time).

All these events were part of the spiritual journey that continued after Bob left his body. Bob's experiences intensified my connection to the spiritual realm, and that connection was with me when I found out two-and-a-half months later that Chris had overdosed on heroin.

When I had first heard about her death, I went uptown to tell my parents that their granddaughter had died. I also wanted to be with them. There was a miraculous moment when my father, who greeted me at the door, came out of his Alzheimer fog for a few minutes. He opened his arms and hugged me warmly and said, "We all did the best we could. Recovery isn't for everyone." Those were the most comforting words said to me in my early grieving for Chris, and they came from my father, who had not been such a comforting person in my life. I was amazed and touched, and then fell into my mother's arms and wept.

The first year after Bob and Chris's deaths was one of intense spiritual experiences—but whether you call it spiritual or magical (like Joan Didion did in *The Year of Magical Thinking*), you will be thinking in ways you may never have thought before, and your experiences will be different and somewhat magical. That is what I am calling awe.

My suggestion is to talk with the person who has died; listen for your loved one's voice (it's not like "hearing voices," but can be an inner sense of a message from that person). Spend time in nature when you can, and look up at the sky. Go out under the night sky and see the stars—you might even pick one that could be your loved one. In general, notice the synchronicity of events. You are in a heightened state of awareness and (I believe) the universe is cooperating with your process in ways you can't understand but can experience.

Here is an example of my awe-inspired or "magical" thinking: My mother died five years ago at ninety-one years of age. It's such a different event when someone dies after having lived out the natural course of his or her life span. My relationship with her felt very complete and it was a lot easier to deal with. She had a good death—she wanted to be in the hospital and was ready to go.

My mother's last year was spent mostly in a recliner in her bedroom. She watched a lot of TV and enjoyed sharing it with me when I visited her twice a week. One of her favorite shows was *Dancing with the Stars*. We watched it together when I came over on Wednesday nights.

My father had died three years earlier of his Alzheimer's disease. She had been devoted to him for sixty-four years. My father was a musician, and they both loved music and entertainment. In the 50s, they had taken Arthur Murray dance classes and loved to dance.

Marie Osmond was on *Dancing with the Stars* just after she had lost her father. She said she pictured her parents dancing in the stars. My mother loved that idea, and we said that she and my father would be doing that together soon. Since her death I sometimes imagine them dancing together when I look up at the night sky and I feel love for them both.

I suggest thinking magically and enjoying it. Breathe life into it, and let it inspire you if you can. It is as real as anything you can touch or taste. You need it right now, and I know it can help you. It helped me and throughout the book I will be describing ways openness and creative thinking can help you through a ruthless grief.

THINGS TO REMEMBER

Permission

Give yourself permission to:

- do things at your own pace and to treat yourself with great care.

- let people help you. They will want to, and you need it.

- rest or sleep as much as you need to.

- cry or not cry in any situation, no matter what you think others are thinking or feeling.

- tell people what you need, including "That doesn't help me right now."

- remove yourself from uncomfortable situations, using phrases like, "Excuse me, I have to . . ."

- feel lost at any given moment and not know what to say or do.

- be alive and practice that on a daily basis.

Shock

- Grief comes in waves; it can be confusing and disorienting. Sometimes you feel okay, sometimes you don't. Ride the waves as best you can.

- You are not going crazy or losing your mind.

- Grief is exhausting. Rest as much as you can, and pace yourself.

- Be careful. You may be numb and disoriented. Move slowly in all areas, both physically and in decision making.

- Let people take care of you. Whenever possible, choose to be around people who have loved the person you have lost.

- Keep busy when you need to—don't let anyone tell you what to do. Suggestions are okay, and accept them as simply suggestions.

- All bets are off—there are no rules for grieving.

Awe

- Give yourself permission to be alive right now. You are the only one who can give it.

- Allow yourself to look for signs of your loved one and believe and even enjoy them. Let those experiences comfort you. They are as real as anything else right now.

- Be as open-minded as you can. Be open to feelings of inspiration and awe.

- You may feel disoriented and filled with a feeling of wonder and otherworldliness—enjoy it, and let it be real for you.

- Trust your intuition—your whole self wants to heal and be whole. Trust the process, and commit to it no matter what.

CHAPTER 2

Rituals: Creatively Honoring the Dead

Rituals are a wonderful part of grieving, and they were a very big part of my ruthless grief for both Bob and Chris, and for my parents as well. In all cases I felt like I was honoring and celebrating them because I was gathering people to support each other and me in each of these losses.

Some rituals are private: an altar at home or looking at photographs and making a collage of them. Most are gatherings with others and can be creative and nontraditional—whatever you wish for in your process of dealing with loss.

PHOTOGRAPHS

Whenever someone in my life has died, I immediately look to photographs to remember them. Seeing the family together and happy, seeing pictures of my loved ones when they were younger, remembering that they had full lives, even if they had been interrupted, was very helpful to my grieving process. My granddaughter, Kaya, studied photography in college, because pictures were so important to her in remembering and processing the ten years she had with her mother and her mother's early death.

Spend time with photos of the deceased as soon as you are able. Many people make up a collage of photos of the person to jog some nurturing memories. Today, the Internet has become a wonderful way to share photos and memories of the deceased. I have heard of memorial pages on Facebook, and I marvel at the creative opportunities they give to honor the dead and share memories of them. Keep pictures of your loved one around your home. Make a special area to honor him or her—an altar, if you will.

ALTARS AND MEMORIAL SPACES

Setting up a little altar at home can be the first ritual. A photo (or many), a favorite object of his or hers, a candle, flowers—these all give a sense of the person you have lost, and they help to honor and represent your loved one early on.

Lighting candles, and incense if you like, can be comforting. These rituals connect me to my Spirit and to a sense of "the Other Side." Maybe it's my Catholic background, but candles create ritual for me, even just my own personal ritual at home. I find the Yahrzeit candle, burning all day and night to remember someone's passing, is intuitively healing.

I recently visited a friend who had lost his dog, Beau, his beloved pet of fourteen years. In the foyer of his house was a table with a picture of Beau, a toy, his leash, and a candle. The memorial was very moving and represented a great love. It honored his spirit to all who entered that home. After a few weeks, when the ashes arrived, my friend moved part of the memorial to the fireplace mantle and left just the photo in the entryway.

Our rituals need to be fluid and creative, and they might keep changing over time as we respond to our needs at each phase of our grieving. The ruthlessness here is in having the courage to break with traditions if they have lost meaning for you, and to be aware of what is appropriate for you personally at any given moment, knowing that your needs will evolve as your grief progresses. I still have a little altar in my bedroom that I started when Bob was sick. It began as a few candles, crystals, and a copy of the St. Francis prayer and has evolved as loved ones have passed. Many different pictures of people who have died have been there—first of Bob, then of Chris and Bob, then of each of my parents, and now of friends or close people who have passed over the years.

I suggest making your home altar your own private ritual. Keep it alive and develop it for yourself with items that have personal meaning for you. I have a piece of black lava that China brought me from Hawaii, where she and her mother lived for several years, and recently Kaya brought me sand from the Mojave desert in Morocco—no memorial there, but it gives me a sense of Spirit and connection with the universe.

The way you honor your loved one is very personal. I used to light a candle at the altar and sit quietly as soon as I got up as a way to honor the dead and honor the day ahead. Now I meditate in other ways, which I will describe in the last section, "Going on Without Them," but early on I suggest sitting with a picture and a lit candle to begin your daily practice of "Permission to be Alive."

Memorials for Those Still Living

Once or twice a year for more than twenty years, I have worked at a therapeutic rehab center called Onsite, near Nashville, Tennessee. I give workshops over a long weekend about codependency and addiction. Recently, one of the primary therapists there was diagnosed with terminal cancer. Everyone rallied around her, and she received a lot of love and care in her dying process. Her friends were planning for her memorial, as her death was imminent, when one of them got the idea to have her memorial while she was still alive and could be there. It was held a week before her death.

People spoke about her life and how many people she had helped and how important she had been to them, and she was sitting right there listening. Her friends and family talked about how much she

41

loved gardening and then took her outside to the memorial garden they had made in her honor. A bagpiper played "Amazing Grace" as she sat in her wheelchair amid the flowers, with her two daughters at her side. Each person went to her, handed her a little colored pebble, and gave her a blessing like "Peace," "Mercy," or "Gratitude," and then placed the pebble in the garden.

I have been to funerals and memorials where the participants have said, "She would have loved this," or "I wish he could have been here to experience this." And then people say, of course, that they were sure he or she was there. But these clever people in Tennessee honored her, expressing their love and appreciation before she left her body. Apparently, she did love it, and she died in peace.

Of course, this is rarely what can happen, but I write about it not only to encourage people to do a living memorial when possible (because I think it's a wonderful idea), but also to encourage you to explore your thoughts about honoring the dead and about dying in open and creative ways. Many possibilities exist.

On the other hand, some ceremonies fall flat and are still important to experience. Last week, a few friends and I went to the beach at dusk to scatter the ashes of our friend, Nancy, who had died a year ago that day. We said a prayer and shouted to the sky, "Goodbye, Nancy." Then we tried to light some Chinese lanterns, but they wouldn't fly because there was no wind.

All rituals are not so moving and successful, but are still important and valuable. My four friends and I honored Nancy in our own way. She was a quirky, creative woman and we had a quirky, creative one-year memorial. Again, giving ourselves permission for our own unique rituals is important.

A friend of mine just told me the story of her father's death. He had always loved Christmas, and he died early on a Christmas morning in Texas. She and her mother were there when he died. They washed the body and put his Christmas presents on him. They opened each one for him and talked to him as if he could enjoy them. She said she felt closer to both her parents than she almost ever had and was pleased she and her mother could share that experience and do that for her dad. I encourage you to "think outside the box" and to give yourself the freedom to create your own rituals whenever possible.

FUNERALS

The religions of the ages exist for a reason, and religious rituals can be wonderful to lean on in times of emotional need, like when someone in our life dies. Within a week of first Bob's and then Chris's deaths, we had a ceremony in a church to honor them.

Try to give traditional rituals like funerals some personal meaning for yourself and others by the way you do them or have them done, or by adding small but meaningful gestures of your own.

I wanted to have a friend play some folk songs and sing at Chris's funeral, but the priest at the church said there was a policy against playing secular music in the church. Instead, my friend played those folk songs at the very traditional funeral home before they closed my daughter's casket. Organizing this personal touch gave me a feeling of involvement and of adding something to the often stiff way that people perform rituals.

There is what I call the "tyranny of tradition" that can take all meaning from the events and leave the griever with mostly resentment and guilt. A Jewish tradition called *avelut* requires a son to formally mourn his parent's passing at temple three times a day for a year. I had a client, Mel, who resented this practice after his father's death because it interfered with his work, his family life, and all leisure activities for one year. He became quite depressed, and I tried to encourage him to have some choice around how often and where he said the prayer. He could not break that commitment or the hold his religious tradition had on him. Although he was able to skip temple a few times, he mostly felt resentful and guilty about the requirement the entire year. His mother is about to die, but he was grateful that they don't have the same tradition for a female death.

I want to be clear that the problem is not with the ritual but with the relationship one has with it. I am sure practicing avelut has helped many people with the depth of their grief, but if the tradition does not suit you, I encourage you to adjust it to have meaning for you personally and to avoid blindly following traditions you might resent.

Ruthless grieving allows you to make independent and even unpopular decisions, to sort out personal meaning from the rituals, and to choose which parts of any tradition will help you and your family and which may not apply. The planning of rituals is up to you, and you can enrich your experience and that of others by your courageous choices.

I recently heard of a Catholic funeral in Florida during which the priest encouraged everyone in the congregation to close their eyes and think of their memories of the deceased. Then he said, "Pick one that represents him the most for you and take that memory into your heart where it can live and flourish in his honor." Then he added, "I encourage each of you to tell someone in the family about the memory so they could know and hear it." That created a wonderful atmosphere of care and communication and bonded the gathering in specific, loving connection.

Before Bob died, I had never planned a funeral or a memorial ceremony. I had attended funerals where the religious aspect was so strong that it seemed more like an infomercial for that religion, rather than a memorial for the person who had died. "Come back to the church—your only protection against death." I have also been offended by hearing a eulogy from someone who clearly had not known the deceased in any way. "It sounds like he was a fine man and will be missed." I knew I didn't want that kind of impersonal, overly religious event.

Pause. Take Three Breaths. Consider: Take a moment to remember any funeral, memorial, or ritual that had special meaning for you, one that stands out as significant, moving, or creative. Think about what made it important to you. Use this information to plan any future rituals or one-year memorials.

Bob's Funeral

When Bob was dying, I asked him if he had any requests for a memorial or if there was anything he wanted me to do after he was gone. He said, "I trust you will memorialize me really well." And I did.

Bob was Episcopalian and much more religious than I. It made sense to choose the church where we had been married for his funeral service. It's a little stucco church with dark red trim and a small bell tower in the center of Bridgehampton, New York. An old friend of Bob's had married us there, and I asked him to do the funeral. Returning to the same setting as our loving, playful, and creative marriage ceremony nine years before only increased my feelings of loss. Bob wanted to be cremated, so there was no casket or wake, for which I was grateful. I didn't want any remnant of my husband's body in the church. It felt too dark and painful. We just exchanged memories of Bob, and I asked several people to give a eulogy.

The minister said I didn't have to speak. He said "This is for you, so just sit back and take it all in." I felt relieved; I was scared enough just showing up at the church. An old friend of Bob's from Nashville happened to be in New York City, so he came out to the East End for the funeral. He was part of a therapy community where Bob had done a lot of training and they'd been quite close. He gave one of the eulogies, speaking beautifully of his love for Bob and focusing on Bob's sense of humor. So did my son, Bill, who had helped Bob a lot throughout his illness. Bill talked about Bob's courage to change his whole life in his fifties by going back to school for his Social Work degree after having been an actor. He admired and loved Bob and honored him well that day. Bob had not had his own children, so his stepson Bill had been extremely important to him. Sadly, Chris was already living on the West Coast, out of touch and homeless, when Bob died. She didn't even know he had died until weeks later.

We also lived in New York City for half the week, so I wanted to have a memorial for Bob there also. I planned it for his birthday on May 22nd, but a month before that Chris died, and there was no way to honor Bob in New York City until the one-year anniversary of his death. More about that later.

Chris's Wake and Funeral

I thought I was being kind to my ex-husband by letting him arrange the funeral for our daughter. The truth is I was probably incapable of doing anything else. I think Chris would have preferred to be cremated, but I was also not up for that battle. A year after her death, on the one-year anniversary, I held a memorial she would have loved.

I've already written in Chapter 1 about how Chris's wake at the funeral home changed my life. I have heard that the tradition of a wake was started before modern medicine; it was the time to sit with the body for a few days in case the person wasn't dead and might wake up. For me, the viewing of Chris's body went far beyond that and was an experience I never could have expected. It was truly a spiritual awakening, and took me by complete surprise.

What changed me most was seeing the body. I hated what she was wearing, (my ex-husband's girlfriend had shopped for it), and I think they even put a rosary in her hand, which made me feel angry. However, none of that mattered after I touched the body. I touched her forehead and kissed it. The cold deadness was unbelievable, but the thought came to me that Chris had gotten the same peace that Bob had. It was a deep, inner knowing that came with a sensation of warmth and comfort. I felt no judgment or failure in her death, only peace. I saw that the body is only a reflection of the Spirit, like a photograph. I saw how beautiful my daughter was on a very deep level, and that she was gone. I cried and cried as I knelt there, and I felt tremendous relief and blessings. No judgments about anything made any sense to me after that. Of course I am not entirely without judgments, but the world has forever been different for me since that moment.

Many people came to give their condolences after I had viewed Chris's body. I don't remember much. I remember the group hug my ex-husband gave to my mother and me. I remember my son being so sad and loving to everyone there. I remember Chris's friends laughing and talking in another room. I remember Chris's ex, Kaya's father, crying like a baby, and I remember loving him for it. I remember China putting her favorite Barbie doll into the coffin before they closed it. Our friend who wrote music and played the guitar played a few songs before the casket was closed and I felt like we were putting music in with her before she left.

The funeral at the Catholic church in Bronxville was challenging for me. I had gone there with my kids before I left my first marriage. We used to go to a folk mass in the basement, which I liked better than the upstairs services. But at Chris's funeral, the church was beautiful, and there were flowers everywhere.

I had woken up that morning remembering the words from the front of Kaya's first communion announcement a few years before. "This is the day the Lord has made; let us rejoice and be glad." The idea of living in the day had been an important part of my spiritual practice, so those words spoke to me. I had decided to speak at the service, and I started my talk with that phrase. I spoke about being grateful for being alive and that I wanted Chris's death to help everyone who was there that day. I wanted everyone there to learn from my daughter's deadly addiction, to let it inform their lives for the better. I needed to speak out about how she had died. People seemed to be moved, and they spoke about my message afterward.

The priest was more personal and warm than I had expected when he spoke from the pulpit. He said to the congregation, "Now you know the name of an angel." I simultaneously thought, "I know the name of two angels," and "They were no angels."

The cemetery service held in the Bronx (and also arranged by my ex-husband) was overwhelming for me. Burying a casket in the ground was so not what I wanted. I knew she was already gone, so I accepted the ritual because I knew it was traditional and what her father wanted. It had no meaning for me except as another opportunity to cry for the loss of my daughter. I remember seeing China and Kaya crying and being right next to them both. The grave of Miles Davis, the famous jazz musician, was nearby, and that gave me a strange comfort knowing Chris's love for music.

ONE-YEAR MEMORIAL

I didn't realize how little memory I had about the time between Bob's and Chris's deaths and afterward as well. I was clearly in shock, but at the time, I didn't really know that.

I strongly suggest having a memorial event for the one-year anniversary of any loss. There is something very significant about that milestone, and I suggest honoring it for yourself and those around you. I think the Jewish tradition has it right about this ritual, which they call an unveiling, when the tombstone is revealed.

That anniversary is also an opportunity to do or say the things that you might have wanted done or said, or to express aspects of the deceased that have come to you over the year. You are much more lucid by that time and will know more of what you need or what might be left undone or unsaid. If you feel complete about the early ritual, you may not need it.

As the months went by, I realized that I had some regrets about each funeral, and I took the opportunity on the one-year anniversary of their deaths to hold a gathering that was more completely to my tastes (and I think to theirs), and to memorialize them more consciously and creatively.

I had been mostly fine with the funeral for Bob, but I still wanted to include other people and to have people speak about him, including myself. For Chris, the one-year memorial was more of an opportunity to redo so much of the religious tradition that had dominated that week and to have an event that would be more to her (and my) liking.

Bob's Memorial

One reason for Bob's memorial was that I hadn't done anything in New York City to honor his passing. We had many friends there, and several people who hadn't been able to make it to the East End on short notice in February of 2001. One of those people was his ex-wife, whom I had never met.

I decided to have the memorial service at a large chapel in the now defunct St. Vincent's Hospital. When we first learned that Bob's cancer had spread, he was in that hospital. I used to go and sit in the chapel in dazed meditation. It looked like a small, traditional Catholic church, but it was on the third floor of a working hospital.

I scheduled the service for the evening of the one-year anniversary of the day he died. I invited eight people to speak about Bob. One was his and my mentor, Tian Dayton. She spoke of her love for Bob and about his fabulous personality. "Every group needs a Bob," she said. A friend of ours who is a composer, David del Tredici, played one of his works on the organ. Our old friend, Anita, who had not been able to get to Bob's funeral, came, and I know the event was important to her.

By the way, it's easy to get mad at people who don't show up for you when you have a loss, but different people are capable of different things. I've heard people say, "You really know who your friends are when something big happens, like a close death." I disagree. Some people missed a beautiful opportunity to connect with Bob before he left, or with the very healing and inspiring gatherings that happened the week after he died, but there is nothing to be gained from judging others or ourselves.

Another group who came to Bob's memorial were some old friends from his childhood neighborhood in Queens. They had been having some reunions for the last several years, and Bob had reconnected with his old teenage friends before he got sick. They loved him, and one of them spoke at length about how on fire Bob had been as a teenager and young adult about acting and the theater. I loved learning more about a part of his life before we'd met.

Bob's ex-wife sat in the back during the service but approached me afterward. She had some old pictures of Bob to give me from when he was in the army. She had left their marriage very suddenly, and Bob had been heartbroken. She had told him at the time, "Someday you'll thank me." He had run into her on the street several years later, after we'd been married a few years. He thanked her. But that day, she thanked me for giving him such a great life, and she said she was happy that he had achieved so much success and personal fulfillment since they had parted.

The whole event painted a picture of who Bob had been on a deeper level than had been possible at the funeral one week after he'd died. And for me it marked the year I had been through, processing and gaining perspective on our relationship and what we had had together. It also was an opportunity to deeply honor this special man with many tributes to his amazing spirit.

Chris's Memorial

Chris was a very nontraditional person, and I knew I needed to do something creative and free-spirited. The rituals of her funeral had felt very different from what she or I would have wanted. I had accepted all the arrangements my former husband had made at the time, and I gained in profound ways from those rituals. However, I still personally needed to have the freedom to create a ritual, an event not Catholic or religious in any way. I wanted it outdoors with lots of music and playfulness. This was the invitation:

Memorial for Chris

A weeping cherry tree grows in my front yard
A gift from friends who wept with me when she died
It was planted with love and is about to bloom there
*   for the first time*
Please come and celebrate Chris's spirit around the tree.
Some of us will sing or dance
Some of us will read a poem or tell a story
Some will play an instrument or beat a drum
The important thing is that you come
And bring your spirit of love and celebration
For the loving soul who left the planet
One year ago now. Please come.

I felt inspired to contact her old friends with whom I had lost touch for many years. Many of them came. I found out that Chris and her husband, Mike, had loved the music that had recently been made popular in the movie *O Brother, Where Art Thou?* and that they had sung it a lot the year they hitchhiked around the country in their early twenties. I think it was Mike who arranged for the minister from Kaya's church (who happened to play the guitar) to come and play those songs. We gathered by the weeping cherry tree that was in full bloom, and he sang those beautiful folk songs. Mike sat next to me on a bench, and we cried together with the music. Another friend of mine, who has a beautiful singing voice, loved Joni Mitchell's music as much as Chris had, and she sang "Seasons" and "Both Sides Now." Seeing and hearing this lovely, spirited young woman singing Joni Mitchell songs in my front yard made me feel like Chris was there singing. I knew she was in spirit.

Earlier that year I had met a young woman at a yoga retreat. She lived in New Haven, where Chris had been born, and she reminded me a lot of my daughter. Her name was Kristie, which had been Chris's childhood nickname. She came over by ferry for the memorial and met and connected with Kaya and China.

It started to rain, and we all went inside to the living room. My brother and his son, Breandan, then seven, played a duet on the piano—so sweet. Some people spoke about how spirited Chris had been from an early age. Two of her closest friends acknowledged how Chris had played matchmaker for them. Her friend Jean said, "She didn't just introduce us, she sold us on each other." They were there with their two children and shared lots of appreciation for my daughter and what she had meant to them.

I knew that I was doing something special to honor my beloved daughter after the dust had settled from the trauma of her death and the way she died. Of course, the whole event was bittersweet. So many friends still alive at her age, so much joy in life, so much sadness and loss—especially seeing her children without a mother. I remember feeling disappointed that the kids chose to mostly be in the backyard playing with Spunky on the hammock. As I look back, I think it was all they could handle.

My Parents' Funerals

Since that time I've had the opportunity to see both my parents die, my father in 2003 at age eighty-six and my mother in 2008 at age ninety-one. Death is not as tragic when people have lived out their natural life spans. There's still grieving to be done, but the memorials I held at the YMCA next to my parents' apartment house had such a different feel. There was a lot of peace and contentment, honoring, and acceptance. My brother and I eulogized them well and had receptions after. The service was small because most of their friends were already gone. They were the last of their generation, and the family had to acknowledge that change. I became the elder in the family and have had to adjust to that new position as well.

Neither my brother nor I felt the need for a one-year memorial as we all felt very complete with both parents' passing and there was just no need. We did gather the family to release their ashes together in the ocean a year and a half after my mother's death (we just couldn't get everyone together before that). My mother had saved his ashes in a container wrapped like a present with a bow and had asked that we scatter them in the ocean with hers. We had a picnic in Montauk on a sunny September day on one of the cliffs over-looking the sea. It was festive and fun. It happened to be my brother's and my son's birthdays, so we even had a cake and sang to them. Kaya was also leaving for college in California the next day, so we were honoring her as well. After lunch we piled into the truck of my son-in-law, Mike, and he drove us down to a giant rock on the shore. There were about fourteen of us. I held my father's ashes and Joe had my mother's. We released them into the ocean in a festive, loving gesture, and we all shouted good-bye to them both. It was a bonding moment for us all, and I think we all knew that they would have loved it and been proud of our little family's way of honoring and releasing them.

Whatever rituals you choose, it's very important to do them the way you want. For public rituals like funerals and memorial services, have people speak who knew your loved one. Speak yourself if you need to or want to. Tell people when you've had enough, or when you need a break. Remember that anger is an early part of grieving and that the rituals often take place early on, so irritation might be present and sometimes even prevalent. When someone close to you dies, many things connected to the rituals and gatherings might annoy you. Please let it all be as it is.

You'll want to be able to say and do whatever you need—ruthlessly—but there are limitations. When and if you get irritated or even enraged by what someone says or does, be sure to grab someone to speak with privately. For example, at the wake when I saw the jumper that my ex-husband's girlfriend had purchased for Chris, I pulled a friend aside and told her what I was feeling. She agreed that Chris wouldn't have been caught dead in an outfit like that. We were able to laugh together, and it relieved some of my irritation and pain. There is a place for gallows humor at all these events, and I encourage it whenever possible. Of course, having available the phrase "That doesn't help me right now" is also a great tool for use at rituals or anywhere there are so many people and so many conflicting needs and wishes. We will discuss managing the angry parts of grief in Chapter 5, Someone to Pin It On.

THINGS TO REMEMBER

- Allow yourself your own private rituals, like an altar in your bedroom, or making a collage of photos to be with and share.

- There is an important place for traditional rituals when a gathering is needed right after a loss.

- I suggest accepting the traditional rituals that are available and already exist. Often much comfort can come from unexpected places and rituals you may never have connected to before.

- The tyranny of tradition can highjack an event. Don't let it if you have any say. Remember that you have choices (more choices than you'll feel you have at the time). You can add small touches to a traditional ritual to give it more personal meaning for you, like a photograph, a song, or a meaningful eulogy. If there's something you need to hear you may have to say it yourself—be spontaneous.

- Be creative about setting up gatherings that have meaning for you. Ask for help as much as you need.

- Add as many personal touches as you can. Give everything the meaning you would wish for.

- The one-year anniversary of your loved one's death, when you are more lucid and have perspective, is a great opportunity to have a ritual more of your own making.

- The one-year memorial gives you even more choices because there are fewer traditional prescriptions on a memorial event held later on.

- Give yourself permission to say or do whatever you need to at the moment, as much as you are able. If you cannot for any reason, pull someone aside so you can express your true feelings, whatever they are.

CHAPTER 3

Warnings: Grieving Can Be Hazardous to Your Health

This entire book concerns itself with warnings about the challenges of grieving. It is a warning not to go unconscious or avoid the process. It is a call to be proactive if you have experienced a close or significant loss.

As a psychotherapist for more than thirty years and as a person in her own recovery process, I have seen many ill effects of unresolved grief. My entire work as a therapist involves issues of unresolved grief: grief for mothers or siblings whose deaths were never faced and dealt with. Of course there are other kinds of losses, but we will be concerning ourselves primarily with how to get through losses as a result of death. There are so many things to learn about the process, many of which will be covered in the sections on the work of grieving in Part Two and going on without the person you've lost in Part Three, but there are some specific pitfalls that need to be identified and clarified before we go deeper. These pitfalls address some specific ways the process of grieving is often avoided or is so distorted that it creates unnecessary suffering and incomplete grief.

I've seen people thrive in their loss and develop in spiritual and emotional ways, and I've seen people whose lives got smaller by going into isolation or addiction, making for much pain and bitterness. None of us want to stagnate forever in our grief; showing up for the process with emotional courage and a willingness to do whatever it takes helps you to move through it and, eventually, even thrive.

RESILIENCE

A popular topic in psychology recently has been the idea of resilience, the quality of bouncing back from severe challenges and getting through traumatic events with grace and ease. Scientists have studied what qualities and behaviors accompany being resilient after trauma or loss.

They have discovered two common traits shared by resilient people. The first is having or building a support group. People who have a strong support group and reach out for help in loss or crisis tend to be more resilient, and they actually can flourish in adversity. We will address this topic in the section about isolation below.

The second quality of resilient people is a positive attitude. People who have a positive attitude and a hopeful outlook on life tend to get through crisis more easily. Our attitude is especially challenged when any major loss has occurred. We tend to feel hopeless and as if we have no future. We can get stuck on the "unfairness" of life and on focusing on all the people who have not experienced the same kind of loss. Of course, we can feel all those attitudes, but it is important to let them move through us and to know we will not always have those feelings. Part of having a positive attitude is being aware of a tendency to compare our situation with others, which often results in us feeling worse about ourselves and sometimes going into a permanent state of self-hatred or blame.

THREE MAJOR PITFALLS IN GRIEF

There are aspects of going through loss that can abort the process and get you very stuck, and there are some particular mistakes to avoid. These are *isolation, medication,* and *comparison*—three very different pitfalls that can lead you into similar, blind alleys with no way out. Basically, they are all ways to avoid the pain of loss, but they result in prolonging the process and ultimately worsening the painful feelings. I would say they even keep you from grieving and instead create suffering.

Isolation

I am a very social person, but after my beloved husband and daughter died, I felt the pull to go off on my own, lick my wounds, and basically never let anyone in again. People die and leave you, so why trust anyone? With great loss comes the feeling that life is just too unpredictable and painful and that continuing to participate in it simply leads to heartache. The natural solution seems to be to close our hearts and never let anyone truly in ever again. Staying away from people is a great start on that strategy.

The other aspect that leads to isolation is a profound self-consciousness, a desire not to be seen or judged for whatever you are doing or not doing at the time. Overcoming this pattern of thinking requires ruthlessness. You don't want a lot of attention at such an emotional time, but actually you have to learn to tolerate some of it so you won't stay totally alone. In my experience, it is extremely rare to be able to travel through grief completely alone. We need care more than ever at these times when we mostly don't want to connect with anyone.

Being a social person, it was probably a little easier for me to let people in and connect with them, but the pull to isolate was still there. However, because I'm a people pleaser, the pull was also there to just go through the motions with others when I was with them and not let them in on my emotional life. This is called emotional isolation. To avoid isolating myself, I had to give myself permission to be ruthlessly honest. I had to learn to cry in front of anyone, to cancel anything and disappoint people, to pick and choose who I wanted to be around. I knew I needed some solitude but in small doses so my negative mind wouldn't take over and drag me under.

Of course you will need some solitude, and you can be alone sometimes. It's just that you will need one or two people to be able to track you and know your whereabouts so you don't get lost in your shock or your sadness and suffer unnecessarily. Ideally, you should have a few people on call. Remember, people want to help you—you just have to ask.

To be around people, I had to be able to tell them, "That doesn't help me right now" when someone I didn't know very well wanted me to know about her late aunt who died in the same city as my daughter, or when someone wanted to let me know that Bob and Chris were in a "better place" when I was in my deepest pain and needed to express it. Not being able to push back with people could have led me into complete isolation.

You can reach out to whomever you choose to be around; you can also choose to not be around anyone you find too difficult or challenging. This will demand being able to take care of yourself around people and ruthlessly telling them what you need. Sometimes it's helpful to contact others who are also grieving. A few months after my losses I met a woman who had just lost her husband. We became fast friends, even though our stories were very different and we were, otherwise, unlikely companions. Going through the feelings of loss together can be very bonding and mutually helpful.

This is true with family members and friends as well. It's often surprising who shows up or who we are drawn to at these times. Don't judge your choices, and let yourself be with who is there or who you intuitively know to contact in your grief.

A few years ago, I helped a man who had just lost all three of his young daughters to a fire. I saw him on about the third day after the tragic events. We set up three little altars in his apartment, and I spoke to him briefly about my own losses. Then I asked who he could call. "Please don't make me see anyone," was his response. I suggested he see just one person. He thought for a while and then said he knew a man who was dying, and he wanted to speak with him. That is the kind of intuition we need to follow in loss. This father was a man with lots of friends, whose voice mail was often full, but he was drawn to talk to this one dying man. That was the beginning of breaking his isolation and beginning to connect with someone who might understand his pain.

This father had contact with someone who was approaching his own death, and it gave him some sense of connection and with what I call the Other Side, just when he needed it. As he learned to give himself permission to protect himself from other people's agendas when he needed to, he was able to see more people.

You need to reach out and then be able to tell people what you need. The ability to set boundaries can help a great deal in feeling safe with people. This includes leaving that person when you are done or need a break.

I had the benefit of being surrounded by friends and family for several months during Bob's terminal illness. Bob was an actor and loved people and attention, so we opened our house to friends and family. Some of those who came to call were people who remained very close to me after he passed on. They were so considerate that I almost couldn't have isolated if I had tried. The support system that helps you through illness can carry you in your grief. Let those people continue to love and support you. Reach out to them. You may have to work hard not to close up and go away from your friends and family. Remember, you can choose to be ruthless. Your grief gives you a free pass, so don't be afraid to use it.

If the person who has died may have been the only close person in your life, you probably feel very untethered, and you need someone to ground you. You both may be awkward and not know what to say. It doesn't matter. Reaching out to others in your time of need is mostly about not being alone. A grief counselor or therapist or spiritual figure in the community may be that person if no one else comes to mind.

Sudden losses from accidents, crimes, or acts of God are a very different situation from death through illness, and they include a more complicated social dynamic. Most social conventions, like perfect manners or more formal ways of planning with people, need to be abandoned after traumatic or sudden losses. People drop in or stay longer than usual, and social conventions often don't apply. All bets are off. Let people come over if you can possibly stand it. You need to be armed with "That doesn't help me right now," or "I need some time alone." But it's good to have someone near you, especially if you live alone, as I did. I had to feel free to go into the other room and let someone just be there in my house or fix me a meal. Lots of unlikely things happen with sudden losses. My friend, Shirley, slept with me in my bed for a few nights after Chris died. A quiet, gentle presence in the house was essential to my peace of mind and feeling at all safe.

Anger

Angry feelings can also feel isolating. Anger is often a part of early grief, so you might feel very irritable when you're not numb. I encourage you to allow it and own it. "I'm feeling a lot of anger right now and don't want to be alone in it. Would you come over?" is a perfectly acceptable statement.

Many people in the cultures of our country (and of many others) are not comfortable with extreme or intense emotions. You will have to be somewhat ruthless to do what you need to do, no matter what other people are comfortable with. You will actually be teaching them about emotions, what intense feelings look like, and how they are expressed, but that is not your concern right now. You will probably have to push through some self-consciousness and discomfort to be around them. Just take a chance and do it. I encourage you to reach out even if you are feeling a lot of anger.

Journaling

Keeping a journal of my feelings about my losses and my process was the most helpful tool I found for my grief, and it relates to not isolating. Emotional isolation can involve isolating from self and remaining unaware of what we are feeling deep inside. "I'm fine" can be a great defense, even from ourselves. It is paradoxical that a relationship with a blank book can be a step in keeping us connected. I had the benefit of having kept journals for years before Bob and Chris died, but you can start at any time. Writing in a journal is like the teenage "Dear Diary" in which one "tells all" to the page. It becomes a relationship with self.

I found that journaling helped with the feelings of isolation and loneliness and even became part of my spiritual practice. "Dear Diary" became "Dear Bob" or "Dear Chris" and sometimes even, "Dear Universe," or "Dear God." Journaling also helped me to clarify what I was feeling and made me feel safer and more comfortable talking to people when I was able.

Medication

Being under the influence of a drug, including alcohol, is a great way to isolate. It creates a giant buffer between you and everyone else, as well as a buffer from feeling the pain of your loss. There is a place for some medication, especially with a sudden or traumatic death. However, there are serious dangers to overmedicating at this point in your life.

There are essentially two types of medicating agents: those that alter long-term mood, like antidepressant medications, and those that act on the psyche immediately, like alcohol or tranquilizers.

Antidepressants

I had a fairly old-fashioned and negative idea about antidepressants until about fifteen years ago, when I had several clients take them and improve remarkably. As their therapist, I found those clients were also more available for doing their therapeutic work, and, despite their pain, had a more optimistic attitude in general. My favorite description of how antidepressants work is that they turn on a pilot light that is dim or has gone out completely. My warning about getting stuck is not about the use of this type of medication. If you suffer from depression or think you might need some chemical help, antidepressants may be recommended. However, in my professional opinion, antidepressants should not be initiated immediately after loss. Wait a few weeks to see where you are. In the first month, some depression and even disorientation are appropriate, and antidepressants won't help that much early on. You need to get through the initial shock before making the decision to use them.

Mood-Altering Substances

I do warn against alcohol and other fast-acting mood changers. Many addictions begin with a loss. Becoming dependent on mood-altering chemicals (not antidepressants) could be a serious risk right now. You might say, "What about ruthless grieving?" or "It helps me to drink right now or live on Xanax or Klonopin." Of course, you get to do whatever you choose, but there are risks, and you need to be aware of them. Becoming chemically dependent at this stressful and vulnerable stage can ruin any dreams you have for the future and can become the narrative of the rest of your life.

You don't want to abort the grieving process. Actually, you will want to, but don't give in to that. I've seen so many people get stuck in chemical dependency after a close loss. I've seen it without losses, but right now you are particularly vulnerable to falling into that hole. After the initial shock, please work at remaining as conscious as you can, and show up for yourself.

If you are someone who isn't addictive and can safely drink, just be aware of the pull to self-medicate, and instead stay connected to people so you don't fall into a long-term dependency on alcohol or tranquilizing drugs. You will not learn anything about yourself or others if you are heavily medicated, and it won't help you become yourself to be able to go on without your loved one in a healthy way.

Now you might have been medicating a fair amount before your loss. You may already be in some trouble with alcohol or pills. You might need to take action. Just stopping is easier said than done. If that's the case, call someone about it—someone who knows you, and also someone who might know something about chemical dependency. If you need to, call Alcoholics Anonymous. Or call a therapist or grief counselor, or a person from a church or synagogue. Call anyone you could begin to trust.

Comparison

Other people's situations or experiences have nothing to do with our own, especially when it comes to grieving. I read recently that the way we grieve is like a fingerprint: there are as many ways to do it as there are people. Comparison—of loss, pain, or time of recovery—is simply not productive. Your pain is your own and must be treated with respect. There is no timetable for grief, so don't use other people to measure what you should or should not be feeling or not feeling.

An irritable and hopeless attitude can be your reality for quite some time. It is a natural phase of the grieving process, but travelling *through* your negative feelings is essential. You have a better chance of righting yourself after you've lost your balance through close loss by avoiding the temptation to compare your pain with others as much as possible and by being aware of the natural tendency to do so.

Comparing your pain to someone else's has several pitfalls, and comparison can interfere with your process of grieving. We can compare situations, feelings, or even the process of grief itself. They are all natural places to go in your grief, but they can get you stuck if you remain unaware of them, and then you cannot move through your feelings or resolve your pain.

How It Looks

Addictions specialist and author Pia Mellody calls destructive comparisons "one up, one down," which means we constantly compare our situation with others and label them either worse than or better than someone else's situation. In either case, we are not with ourselves or our own experiences. In grief, this can come in the form of "My pain is worse than anyone else's," or "My pain isn't as bad as other people's (who are doing better than I am)." These are destructive thoughts. There is no comparing pain.

We tend to compare our own internal experience of pain with how other people look in their loss. We always come up short when we do. We actually have no idea how anyone else is experiencing the world, but if we go by how something looks, it's never good for us. Even when we look like we're doing better than other people, we are still comparing, and that comparison tends to distort our focus on our own experience.

Be aware of thoughts like "I shouldn't be feeling like this," "My sister seemed to spring back so quickly," or "I only lost one person, not my entire family like other people have." Become more ruthless on your own behalf. A sure way to block your process is to compare your pain or even your situation to that of anyone else. Awareness is the key. When you can recognize your thoughts of comparison, the weight of their destructive influence goes away.

Feeling Sorry for Yourself

After Bob and Chris left, I felt very sorry for myself—which was appropriate to the situation. Rather than calling it "feeling sorry for yourself," I called it "feeling for yourself," which is just compassion for your own experience. However, I did tend to ask, "Why me?" which is a natural question that often has no good answer. Some of the negative answers I came up with were "I am being punished," "I didn't deserve them in the first place," or even, "Something I did or said may have caused their death." But in the course of speaking with others I respected, I decided, "Why not me?" People have lost husbands and offspring since the beginning of time, and now it had happened to me, like it was my turn in the barrel. This realization shifted parts of my attitude from negative to positive and helped with some of the self-recriminating thoughts so I could show up for the grieving process, whether I liked it or not. And mostly, I didn't like it.

Grieving the "Right" Way

In his book *Unattended Sorrow,* grief counselor Steven Levine describes the risks of not attending to or completing the grieving of our losses. In the first chapter, he writes that he discovered that most people who have lost a loved one think they are not grieving in the "correct" way. The question often is, "Am I doing it wrong?" And the corollary to that would be, "Everyone else is doing it better than I am." Actually, you get to "do" it however you need to. That is one of the points of calling grieving "ruthless." Do what you need to do, no matter what others think or do. Give yourself permission to be how you are and to do or feel what you feel guided to do or feel. It is your unique process, and you need to find your way.

I have always loved what Levine wrote. I've used that idea myself, and I passed it on when I was helping people through losses. His concepts are part of what led me to use the term *ruthless* to describe effective grieving. My own experience has taught me that one must do whatever one needs to do to get through this giant adjustment and emotional upheaval. Stand up to people who think otherwise; listen to them when it feels right. There is an intuition toward healing that can be very strong—follow yours, no matter what.

Do not compare your own timing and depth of feeling with how you think you should be grieving, either. Sometimes when a wave of grief would sideswipe me, my thought would be, *I thought I was doing so well.* I didn't realize I was *still* doing well, and a wave of intense feeling didn't mean I wasn't. How long you remain in intense feelings is also individual. Some people just take longer than others—and there should be no judgments about that.

Inability to Cry

Another pitfall of comparison is that many people cannot access their tears for a long time. They get frozen; this feature is especially true with a sudden loss and is a part of the shock. Being numb is a part of being in shock, and feeling numb lasts as long as shock does. "I should be feeling more right now. "Everyone is watching me and seeing that I'm not crying. I'm weird." People don't focus on us as much as we think they do, and they judge us much less than we often believe or than we judge ourselves.

Relief

When someone who was very difficult for us dies, we can fall into comparison. I had a friend who lost her husband the same month Bob died. However, their marriage had been dead long before he died, but they had both stayed, living in deep resentment and alienation. They had children and religious beliefs that kept them together and kept them stuck. When my friend's husband died, she felt nothing but relief. She went to grief groups and felt totally alienated because she had no sadness in her. There is no comparing pain or lack of pain. There is no comparing the amount of expressed emotion or lack thereof. The grief process can teach us a deeper respect for everyone's way of doing things, for their emotional styles, and their timing of going through their process. It did that for me and I needed that respect for myself.

SIDE WITH YOURSELF

A big part of ruthless grieving is being on your own side, no matter what. This attitude can help prevent you from making negative comparisons about your grieving process. Everyone's grief is different, and we each must find our way in our own time, finding the intuition and tone that fits for each of us.

I often use the phrase "side with yourself" in counseling people who have many different issues. I developed this idea from sitting with so many people in therapy whose narrative was about how other people felt or thought about them. I had also personally experienced worrying about someone else's perspective instead of my own. "What would they think about what I am doing right now?" or worse, "What would they think about what I am feeling?" are examples of this type of thinking. There is no more important "side with yourself" situation than when you are grieving.

There is also a kind of distortion in relationships in which we tend to overidentify with other people. "Your pain is my pain" can lead to much confusion and unnecessary suffering. There is no more profound example of that than when someone close to you dies. We tend to overidentify with the deceased and suffer unnecessarily with their imagined experience of death. Recently, a friend of mine in his late seventies lost a lifetime friend to a botched heart procedure. He couldn't get rid of the image of his friend drowning in his own blood. I suggested to him that he had no idea how his friend did or did not experience death and that he didn't need to suffer in that way. I suggested he tell himself, "I am alive and he is not." Finding a way for that to be okay often takes some practice. Giving yourself permission to be alive is siding with yourself in a very profound and meaningful way.

"Side with yourself" means you don't compare yourself to anyone else or let anyone criticize you in your grief. Now is not the time to worry about what people will think. In grieving, it is so easy to take someone else's side or to make up what someone else is thinking or feeling about us. We are often fearful or uncertain in this new situation, and it is very easy to turn against ourselves in self-doubt or fear.

Do not compare your pain to anyone else's. Don't compare your feelings and how you are or are not expressing them. Every loss is different, as is every person's way of experiencing it. Permission to be how you are right now, "on your own side," can go a long way in getting you through this complex journey.

THINGS TO REMEMBER

Three things could abort your grief and keep you stuck in it.

Isolating

- You need people right now, even though you will want to be alone.

- Let people in slowly, and tell them what you need—they want to help you.

- Reach out, especially if you live alone or tend to isolate anyway.

Medicating

- Be aware of the dangers of overmedicating.

- Antidepressants are okay at certain stages, but don't begin too early.

- Don't get hooked on pills or alcohol. If you tend to self-medicate, a good time to reach out for help is during the grieving process.

Comparing

- Don't let anyone shut you down with control or criticism—there are no rules for grief. Don't let anyone tell you how you should be right now.

- Don't compare yourself and how you are feeling or doing with anyone else's process.

- "Side with yourself" can be a positive attitude that helps.

Give yourself permission to grieve the way you feel guided to do it:

- The way we grieve is like a fingerprint—everyone has his or her unique way of doing it.

- Cry when you need to. Don't if you don't. Feel what you feel, and let yourself have your own pace.

- Work at remaining as conscious as you can.

CHAPTER 4

Feeling Lost: Giving Yourself Permission

We've all heard these common expressions: "She would feel lost without him." "I would be lost without my kids." "If my daughter died, I don't know what I'd do—I'd be lost." These are all true statements. The people we love anchor us to our lives and our sense of self and the world. Without them, we often feel very lost.

I have been committed to growing as a person and being the best person I could be since I was in my thirties. I considered myself a seeker and had done a lot of emotional and spiritual work. I had a good education, a full and rich life, work that I loved, and a spiritual practice. However, faced with the death of my husband, I did feel lost and was even surprised at how disoriented I was. Then the death of my daughter happened so soon after, and I was beyond lost.

"I'm lost without them" took on a whole new meaning. I was lost without my husband and then without one of my two offspring being alive on the planet. *Lost*. Thank goodness for social skills and knowing how to "go through the motions" in my early life. "I can do this" was something I told myself often—and I could, but I had to find the ruthless parts of me that could fiercely persist no matter what.

MY FIRST YEAR OF GRIEVING

Bob died on February 6, 2001. By April, I was back to work and planning on renting my house for the summer when I learned that Chris had overdosed. May is a blur, but I was seeing clients for sessions and going to 12-Step meetings. I made those meetings my grief group and let it all out in sharing—often.

The summer of 2001 was better. I live in Sag Harbor, New York, because I want to be by the sea in the summer. I spent lots of time with my granddaughters, Kaya and China, at the beach. Spunky, Bob's dog, was our constant companion. My son, Bill, was around a lot and had just started to date his future wife. They invited me to some fun Hampton events, and I went. Signs of life were all around me—summer, kids, my dog, my son starting a new romance. There were glimmers of light shining more and more through the scrim of my tears. I felt very connected to the sky and imagined both Bob and Chris up there. I wrote in my journal every day, including many letters to both of them.

The twin towers of the World Trade Center came down on 9/11 that year. I was in the West Village in New York City and saw a small fire in the first tower, and like many others, I thought it was just a small plane accident. When the towers came down, I remember thinking that my own two towers had come down earlier that year. In the aftermath I felt like the world was catching up to how I had felt when Bob and Chris died. I came up with the idea of the "unheroic death" (discussed in Chapter 8) because of all the heroic stories that ensued after 9/11 and how different I felt about the way Chris died of a drug overdose.

Fall is always hard for me. I suffer from seasonal affective disorder, otherwise known as SAD. As the days get shorter and shorter, I get sadder and sadder. Of course, my SAD intensified that fall. My father's Alzheimer's was progressing, and I started spending more time with him and my mother. She was bereft about him, and

I was in my losses. We bonded more than we ever had since I was little.

I don't remember the holidays much that year. I remember people were really nice to me, and I felt like a mental case. I couldn't exercise or go to yoga. It was even hard to read. Everything felt like an effort, but I did something every day. I couldn't be alone, so when I wasn't with people my journal was my constant companion. I planned Bob's one-year memorial for February, and I got very involved in it.

I went on a yoga retreat in St. John in January with my friend Susan. I started to get my body back and to feel more alive. I met a young woman there whose name was the same as Chris's childhood nickname: Christie. She looked a lot like Chris, and I befriended her. She even came to Chris's one-year memorial in April. My connection with her was beyond words, and it helped me. I told her how much she reminded me of my dead daughter, and we both cried. Meeting her made me feel like the universe was caring for me, a good sign that I would be able to go on without my beloved daughter.

I planned and held the one-year memorials in February and April. They were what I lived for during those months when I felt I had no purpose.

Lost for Words

Simple things like meeting someone new were a tremendous challenge then, and I frequently felt lost about what to say when asked about my family. I dreaded the question, "Do you have children?" If I said, "Yes, I have a grown son" (which I did sometimes to protect myself from other people's reaction), I felt like I was betraying Chris (and myself). If I told the questioner about Chris, it was a big story that affected people deeply, and then I had to deal with their reactions to it. "Yes, I was married, but he just died." is a conversation stopper. I felt like a pariah. Losing someone can be a giant reason not to go out and meet new people. Just the social awkwardness alone is enough reason to isolate. And then there are all the feelings that come up in telling your story when you are with people you don't know very well. It's painful and often feels too difficult.

I tried saying I had a son, or I wasn't in a relationship, but it felt awful. Over time it became much easier, and now I say what I feel comfortable saying at the moment, which is sometimes a lot, sometimes a little, and sometimes nothing at all.

I had the additional challenge of explaining how Chris died in such a shameful way. Even today, I make a point to tell people how she died because I have always wanted her death to help others. So as awkward as it felt and still feels sometimes, the conversations have led to many interesting discussions, and people often open up about their own experience of addiction or death.

There is a saying in the 12-Step literature that encourages us to remember that no matter how painful or "how far down the scale" our story is, it can benefit others. Developing an open attitude about sharing my experience and choosing to do so helped me to connect with people and the world, as I learned over time to negotiate my internal lost feeling and my external alienation.

We find ways to tell as much as we choose—which is sometimes nothing at all. And we find ways to tell ourselves whatever we need to hear. The most socially daring way I have heard about dealing with this was from a woman who lost her teenage daughter last year. She practiced telling people, "I have two children: a son, who is here, and a daughter, who is in the spiritual realm." When you're grieving, it's good to know you can say whatever you need or want to say— to be ruthless. I have heard of a Native American tribe that says of people who have died, "They walk the other world." When you've had a close loss, it can definitely feel like they walk the other world. However, saying it is another matter, and is just one of your many options in dealing with people.

Lost in Social Situations

The social aspect of loss is just one way that a close loss affects us. Being with other people can be so difficult. Sometimes, if I was feeling angry in my grief, I would tell about the deaths very directly, knowing I would purposely affect the questioner. Sometimes if someone was complaining about their grown kid or their spouse, I would say, "At least they're alive." That was ruthless grieving coming out in negative ways, but sometimes I didn't care.

It is a delicate balance to negotiate being socially appropriate and true to yourself at the same time. All bets are off. You get to find your own way in the sometimes harrowing landscape of dealing with other people when you are having so many conflicting feelings of your own.

Pause. Take Three Breaths. Consider: What do you wish you could say to people about where you are at right now? How much have you told them? How daring do you want to be with people socially? Would you like to take more risks?

My friend David told me recently that when he had back surgery and had to use a cane, he felt protected from people on the street or in the subway—so much so that he admitted to carrying it far beyond needing the support to walk. He used it to signal to other people that he was in a sensitive state and needed extra consideration.

This extra consideration is an important thing to ask for when you're grieving. Be ruthless about what helps you and what doesn't. If you need an outward symbol that says, "I'm vulnerable right now," don't hesitate to use one.

I have long been interested in the custom of wearing black when someone dies. This social signal that the person is in mourning or "at a loss" lets people know they may need special consideration or treatment. Queen Victoria popularized the custom in her long grief for her husband, Prince Albert, in the middle part of the nineteenth century. This custom was also reduced to simply the wearing of a black armband to signal a close death. Some say it was to honor the dead, but most agree it was for the griever to signal his or her state of mind and spirit, and a silent request for extra care and respect from the outside world.

I've often wished we practiced that tradition in our culture. My black band would have signaled to the world, "I am in an altered state; I have faced death at very close range, and it has taken a loved one. I'm a little lost right now, so please treat me with extra care, with kid gloves, if you will." Like David did with his cane, I might have worn an armband longer than the traditional one year just to prolong a sense of safety and care from those around me.

What would your black armband say to the world? Maybe you wouldn't want to be seen in that light. Maybe it would make you feel too vulnerable. If you've suffered a loss, my suggestion is to psychically put one on for yourself as a reminder to treat yourself with kid gloves and that you are probably more vulnerable and sensitive than you have been at other times in your life. You probably have special needs that are easy to forget or that could go underground and be lost. So put on the armband in your mind's eye, decide what you'd like to signal to those around you, and proceed with your year or more of grieving.

YOUR INTERNAL LANDSCAPE

Not knowing what to say with others is only one form of feeling lost. "Who am I without them?" is the deeper question you initially won't know how to answer.

My son, Bill, gave me a book when Bob died. It was *A Grief Observed* by C. S. Lewis. It was the first written help I received. What stood out to me was Lewis's statement that he never knew grief felt so much like fear. That helped me a lot; it was part of how

I began to accept feeling so lost and developing the idea of needing to be ruthless to get through my losses. Losing someone in your life is frightening, and we need a lot of extra care to proceed in healthy ways. The book also gave me the idea of observing my grief by writing it down, which helped me enormously throughout.

Sometimes I didn't know who I was after my husband and daughter were gone. Over time, of course, this changed, but my mind went everywhere, and not to positive places. I recently heard someone giving a spiritual talk say, "My mind doesn't give a shit about me." Your mind can say the meanest things, and that is especially true in close loss. There is a great need for developing positive self-talk, which we will address in more depth in the next section, "The Emotional Work."

Talking to Someone Who Has Died

My internal landscape was where I began to heal—a prayer, a loving thought of Bob or Chris, or a warm memory helped ground me. I thought a lot about what they would want for me and made myself remember loving moments with them and remember that they were fine right now. They walk another world. I developed a sense of them being with me. That changed a lot over time also, but was very comforting early on in my losses. I had to learn to focus on and take care of myself.

In the course of my own therapy work before their deaths, I had found that writing in a journal helped me in many different ways. I always reference the teenage model of "Dear Diary." I'll explain.

As we develop through our teenage years, we need to establish a sense of identity. "Who am I?" is the question we ask ourselves as adolescents. Many teenagers write in a journal regularly to process their sense of self and their relationship to the world around them. I had to do that emotional work in my thirties, as I hadn't fully differentiated, or developed a separate identity from my parents as a teenager or young adult. This same process of concretizing your relationship with yourself can be very important to your grieving. As a writer, that modality speaks to me and helped me develop a sense of being a separate person from Bob and from Chris in the deepest part of my grieving. Yours may be painting or listening to music, but journaling can be so helpful because it puts words to our experiences with and without our departed loved ones, to our sense of self, and to our wishes and wants for our future life.

In the next section, I will describe several different kinds of journaling exercises that can help you complete and resolve the relationship, deal with feelings of regret, guilt, and shame, and build a new sense of self and of life with others. Writing yourself a new place inside yourself and the world is one way you can begin to define your new internal landscape.

BEHAVIORS OF LOSS

A friend of mine told me a story she said she had only told one other person because she was so embarrassed about what she had done. A very close friend of hers had died in a plane crash on the way to visiting her in New York. My friend left her office and went home as soon as she heard the news of her friend's death. She didn't know what to do, so on impulse she called 911—and within minutes there was an ambulance outside her house. She felt embarrassed, but the EMTs were very kind to her and stayed with her for a while until she felt a little safer and could call a friend to come and be with her.

With a close loss, sometimes our thinking and behavior don't make much sense, and they may even defy logic completely. I heard an interview of a mother who had lost two of her children in a car crash. She said that for several weeks she would be up at night searching the house for her little girls. Her family would try to remind her of what had happened, but in the middle of the night she could not hear it. In the morning she would remember again, but that nighttime behavior continued for weeks.

Bob had a brother and sister-in-law whose teenage daughter was hit by a train while she ran across the tracks. For more than a month after this tragedy, Bob's sister-in-law, the girl's mother, would prepare a daily meal, take it to the grave, and bury it there. Bob's brother would take her there but was aware of how irrational his wife's behavior was. Gradually, her bizarre but understandable behavior of preparing food for her daughter in the grave ceased, but her husband remembers doing it with her and how upset he was about it.

These are examples of the type of odd behaviors that can happen in early grief. It's important to let yourself, or your grieving loved one, perform certain behaviors, to play them out, until they no longer need their denial or resistance to face the reality of death and loss.

Searching and Longing

There is a very common experience of thinking you see your lost loved one in a crowd or on the street. It happened to me most on the street; I'd catch just a glimpse of someone, reminding me of Bob or Chris. Bob had a mustard-colored winter jacket, and that jacket seemed to be everywhere when I would go out that winter. I would catch my breath, and for a moment I would believe it was Bob. I would want to follow the person, even after I knew it wasn't him. Then the harsh reality would hit, as if I'd forgotten he was gone, and I'd feel the pain. Over time those "sightings" became less surprising and would sometimes even bring me some comfort. "He walks the other world," I would remind myself. With Chris, the smell of patchouli or the sight of a woman with dreadlocks would make my heart race. It happens much less often now, but I find it comforting when it occurs. It feels like a reminder of her existence—she walks the other world.

Breaking Traditions

My friend James uses the phrase *soup sandwich* when he talks about being messy or disorganized. I was a soup sandwich for several months after my losses. I think we need a lot of permission early on (and even later—for at least one year) to be however we are to get through and heal from a loss. I often think of the tyranny that traditions can become, and I encourage everyone I encounter to question their traditional thinking (with or without a loss). Make individual decisions about your choices and behaviors according to your own values at the time, rather than following traditions in a blind or unconscious manner. For example, I gave myself permission not to respond to people's cards and letters of condolence for either loss. This was unlike me, but I just couldn't muster the energy to do it. Many people get a lot of solace from responding to those condolences, but I needed to not do so, and I don't regret my decision. This is the kind of permission you need to give yourself: to break with tradition and find your own way when you are experiencing loss and feeling lost.

Returning to Work

In the first months after my losses, I both took it easy a lot and worked fairly hard. I've always liked the phrase "Work Hard, Play Hard," but this was more like "Rest Hard, Make an Effort Hard." There can be a lot of pressure about how much or how little one works immediately after loss and beyond. Working as a therapist was good for me because it constantly gave me new perspectives, although early on I sometimes struggled with them. I would come to a session after writing in my journal and sometimes crying, to sit with someone who was stuck in a bad marriage or fighting with a brother over money. I would think, *Really?* I have always looked at sessions with people in the light of the question, "What can I learn from this?" and I learned a lot in the sessions I had with clients in 2001. I had a different perspective on what was important and would gently share it where appropriate. I'm sure my work changed a lot during that time as I felt a strange combination of total compassion for the human condition and a distinct perspective that transcended all pain. Whatever my view, I kept going, and clients seemed to get better.

I am someone who loves my work, and it has been a big part of my life since I started doing therapy in the 1970s. However, everyone's relationship with work is different. How soon you return to it is a very individual decision. Even if you love your work, you might decide you need a lot of time away from it before you resume.

Woody Allen's philosophy that "showing up is 90 percent of everything" can be very helpful when you're grieving. Even though I didn't know what I was doing half the time, I showed up and let my experiences change me.

I am generally encouraging you to be quite permissive with yourself when you are in this kind of pain. I have found that gentleness and compassion are the most needed attitudes and help the most in travelling through the landscape of deep loss. I have discovered one permission to be most important. It is permission to be alive, and it is salve on the wound of any survivor guilt that may be present in your grief.

PERMISSION TO BE ALIVE

I wrote earlier about Permission to be Alive, but I want to emphasize its importance around feeling lost. It is my experience that we don't recognize the desperate need for that permission in early grief because we mistake the deathly feeling of survivor guilt with the pain of grief. We'll explore that more in a moment.

After Bob died, I would say, "It's okay that I'm alive while he is not," but I found that felt like I was saying it was okay that he was not alive, and it definitely wasn't okay. Finding the right words can be an empowering part of your grieving process, so make up your own words if mine don't suit you. The important thing is to find the words that can help you give yourself permission to be alive on the planet even though someone you love has left his or her body.

It doesn't usually happen all at once, but as you practice your daily Permission to be Alive, your life force can gradually get stronger, and you'll begin to get your bearings from day to day.

Survivor's Guilt

When I realized that I needed permission to be alive after Bob died, I first understood what we call survivor guilt. I didn't know I was feeling guilty to be alive, I just knew I felt like death myself.

There was a strong pull to go with him. It's the nature of attachment to be with the person we are attached to. I had to accept gradually that I couldn't go with him and that the gift of having a human life still existed for and in me.

When Chris died, I was more out of it and not as conscious for several weeks. The shock and awe took over, and I was much more lost. I felt so confused that she had grown in me and come out of my body and that her flesh was not alive anymore. I had given her the gift of life, and she had lost it. How could I go on if she was not on the planet? It's a parent's job to keep her child alive, and I had failed.

The guilt I felt was specific and intensely distorted.

It was much more difficult after her death to give myself permission for my own life. I didn't get the immediate relief I had felt on Susan's table about Bob. I went back to Susan, but all I could do was cry and cry about the fact that Chris was gone.

For several years before either death, I had developed a practice of deciding in the morning to be grateful for the day I was about to experience. In 12-Step addiction recovery, this is called the Third Step. Each morning (when I remembered) I would make the decision to live that day with an awareness of the Love that was available to me. I would decide that the world was full of care that could guide me through the next twenty-four hours. It is a spiritual practice that helps people heal from the darkness of addiction and a negative lifestyle.

I didn't feel any of that after the profound loss of Chris and the shock of her death. Except for the fact that friends and family were showing me love on a daily basis, I was unable to feel positive about the world.

I did continue to practice the Third Step (when I remembered it) even though the idea felt empty and meaningless. Gradually I began to feel my life force return. That happened most often when, having made the decision to live the day, I spent time with Chris's two young daughters, Kaya and China. I remember being on the beach with them the summer after Chris died and feeling grateful to be alive for the first time in months.

Eventually I came up with the words, "It is okay that I am alive and they are not." I encourage you to say those words, even when you don't feel them: "It is okay that I am alive and they are not." In the beginning it definitely does not feel okay that your loved one is not here. And how could it be okay that you are here alone? You might want to change the wording to suit your own loss, but basically you will need to find a way to affirm your life force in the face of your loss and decide to live in each day as best you can. In the morning, as soon after awakening as possible, I suggest you give yourself permission to be alive, just for that day.

One Day at a Time

Just focusing on living in this day alone has always helped me, and it has since I started doing it in the 1980s. However, in the face of losses (or really any of life's challenges), living "one day at a time" has helped me get through those most difficult days.

Early in the grieving process we have to shift and change our attachment to the one who has died—not break it, exactly, but shift into a more spiritual or ethereal connection, something beyond the senses. Some people might consider that breaking an attachment, but for me that meant a transformation into a different kind of bond. For a while I was confused between who Bob and Chris were and who my Higher Power or God was, as if they felt like my "God" for a time. Later on I had to differentiate more between them, but eventually I decided they were with or in my sense of God.

We will speak more about this later, in the deeper emotional work of Part Two. For now, I want you to know you can work on the idea of going on without your loved one by practicing permission to be alive on a daily basis. I encourage you to find your own words if mine don't suit you. Decide what it is you need to hear, and tell yourself those ideas in your own words. No one can give you permission to be alive but you.

In Part Two, we move on to the deeper emotional work of grieving and processing your loss. Whether in three weeks, three months, or three years or more after your loss, you need to go through the feelings to come out the Other Side more whole and resolved that they have left their bodies and you have not. It is my experience that when we have resolved our grief, all that is left is Love—the love for them that we experienced while they were alive, the acceptance of the connection with them however loving or unloving it had been, the love and forgiveness of self and of every other being alive or dead.

Whether you need to search for your loved one in the street sometimes or bury food at his or her grave, pray to your loved one as if he or she were a saint and ask for help, or believe that person is in heaven or in a paradise where you will eventually be together, grieving ruthlessly allows you to break some rules and traditions. If it suits you, make some decisions that other people may not like or understand, forget about what other people may be thinking about you and your grief, and give yourself complete permission to find your way through this messy bog.

Armed with your journal, the practice of your daily decision to be alive, and some leap of faith about your intuition and belief in healing, you are ready to move into the work of the deepest part of grief.

THINGS TO REMEMBER

- Give yourself permission to feel lost, no matter how strong you have felt in the past.

- Get a journal and begin to write in it. Frequently.

- Give yourself permission to say or do what you want or need about your loss.

- Protect yourself from other people's expectations of what you need to do or not do.

- You may find yourself doing odd things like thinking you spot your loved one on the street or talking to that person as if he or she is still with you. This is perfectly normal.

- Give yourself permission to break with some traditions of grieving if they don't suit you.

- Survivor guilt is real and needs your attention.

- Give yourself permission to be alive on a daily basis. I suggest telling yourself, "I am alive and they are not" in whatever words suit you.

PART TWO

The Emotional Work

CHAPTER 5

Blame and Healthy Anger: Someone to Pin It On

After the numbness and denial pass, anger is a natural response that wells up in the person who is mourning loss. It doesn't always occur, but is often prevalent in early loss. People get angry when someone they love leaves. When we get frustrated, we usually experience anger. And there is nothing more frustrating than someone in our lives disappearing.

Immediately after Bob died, I wasn't that aware of my anger because he had such a loving and peaceful death, for which I'd had a lot of time to prepare. However, even though I'd had three months of knowing he was leaving, when I was at the train station with Shirley, my statement, "I am done with him," came up in me out of the blue when I wasn't even aware of feeling angry.

PASSING THE BLAME

Anger continued to be a theme through the next several months. I was angry at God, at death itself, at the doctors who couldn't save him, at Bob, and sometimes at other people in his family who had not been as healthy but were still living. Sometimes, I would feel angry with couples who were both still alive.

I needed someone to pin Bob's death on; someone had to be

responsible for this injustice. His death felt like a big mistake on God's part. Sometimes I felt punished, and then I'd be even angrier with God. My ex-husband was still alive, and my beloved Bob was gone. My former husband took the heat of my internal wrath—but because we weren't even in much contact, I certainly wasn't going to express that to him.

I was mad at Bob for leaving me. Why would he do that? Eventually, I figured out that he hadn't wanted to leave, but before that, I was pissed. Even if he hadn't meant to leave me, I felt angry. I felt the burden of having to take care of everything myself, and I didn't like it.

Pause. Take Three Breaths. Consider: How angry do you feel about this loss? Where does your anger want to go? Are you blaming your loved one, yourself, the doctors, others involved in the situation, or God?

Financially, I felt very alone and abandoned, and I was angry about that. I felt somewhat victimized and put upon to have to take care of my finances alone. We had bought a house together and rented an apartment in New York to work there half the week. The overhead was high, and Bob had been very generous and fair about sharing the cost of everything. Now, I had to do it all myself. I actually rented out a room in both places to a friend, or in the case of our New York space, a friend of a friend. I felt a little like a martyr. I was left angrily wondering who would continue the routines that had made up our lives. Who would go to the dump, and who would walk Spunky?

Thankfully, my anger about Spunky subsided first. I would walk Spunky, our black and white cocker spaniel, around the block in the West Village. I would sense Spunky's innocence and that he missed Bob, too, and I'd feel a lot of warmth and comfort. Walking Spunky became a connection with Bob. He had deeply loved that dog. I felt it when I walked him, and it turned into warm feelings of love for both of them.

The anger after loss can feel so random and irrational, because mostly it is. I could have resented Spunky for years—I'd never wanted that dog, and when we got him, Bob had agreed to do all the work. He did, at first, but then I grew to love our little puppy a lot, and although Bob had done the lion's share of the work, we had balanced out the job of his care a little more.

Early on after Bob's death, phone solicitors also took the brunt of my wrath. Around dinnertime, the phone would ring and a solicitor would ask, "May I speak with Robert Chambers?" Sometimes, I would be so glad to hear someone calling him, but hearing something like, "We have a special offer . . ." would earn the reply, "He's dead," or "He just died." I would take some perverse pleasure in upsetting the caller on the other end. It was not my finest hour, but that was part of my ruthless grieving. The truth is sometimes I still respond that way if I'm upset about something else and one of those calls comes in. Mostly, I'm especially nice to telephone solicitors as a way of making up for my ruthless behavior from the past.

Who Is to Blame?

Common objects of anger are the doctors who took care of loved ones. Bob's doctors had operated to remove a large, cancerous tumor and his left kidney, and they said they had "gotten it all." Three months later they checked his lungs and said there were small spots. It turned out the cancer had spread to his brain. In fact, his cancer had spread all over his body, and they hadn't checked for it immediately after the surgery.

A few people suggested suing the doctors. I had no interest in expending energy against Bob's doctors, but many people do. It provides an extreme outlet for anger, gives the grievers someone to pin death on, and helps delay the emotional work necessary. In general,

I don't recommend it. I guess it can be a part of ruthless grieving, and there are, of course, cases of severe malpractice that warrant legal action. Whatever you feel or do about your doctors, it is important to be aware of the anger involved in grief, and where you choose to direct it.

I heard recently of the death of someone's great uncle at ninety-two. His widow blamed the doctor for mishandling his case and is threatening to sue. This I would discourage. The widow was looking for someone to blame, but I think pausing and being conscious of her attitudes and feelings about her husband living for ninety-two years might help ameliorate her rage at her dear husband's death.

Don't expect your anger to make a lot of sense. It often will not, even to you. It just is. When a friend of mine lost her son recently in a helicopter crash, she said the anger about his death was the only thing that kept her upright, but she had no intention of feeling anger toward him in any way. Anger and blame can be a kind of fuel for a while that can keep you motivated when you really just want to collapse.

Anger can just bubble up, no matter what the situation. A friend of mine remembers how angry her mother was at her stepfather when he died. She kept saying, "How dare he die like that? I took such good care of him." They were German Jews and had lived through World War II together, so her mother was especially affronted that he would die and leave her after all that they'd gone through together.

When Chris died, I felt that my rage was even more justified. How could God take my daughter from this earth? Because of her addiction and her living so far away, my connection with her was down to feeling grateful she was alive on the planet. Her connection with me was down to a collect call about once a month. I couldn't refuse them.

Attending 12-Step meetings after her death felt bittersweet. People who had been addicts and were working to recover from their addictions surrounded me. I would hear of miracle after miracle about someone hitting rock bottom and ending his or her use of drugs or alcohol, and then going into recovery and getting better. Whenever I heard statements like, "Now my life is full of blessings, I have my kids and family back, and I am grateful," every emotion—from jealousy to anger to intense sadness—would course through my body. I had felt anger over the course of Chris's addiction, when she would travel far away and abandon her girls—again. After she died, I remember someone sitting next to me at a meeting telling me he was uncomfortable sitting next to me because he could sense so much pain in me. It didn't feel good to hear, but on some level I felt validated and some compassion from him at the same time.

When someone seems complicit in her own demise, the situation is fraught with additional rage as well as other intense emotions. I was furious with Chris for dying, and so mad at the universe for her death. It felt so random and unnecessary.

But she was my daughter, and I felt a lot of compassion and empathy for her as well. I had worked a lot to keep remembering that she had an illness as lethal as a cancer, but after she succumbed to it, I had no understanding or reasoning at all. I was just angry at everyone and everything.

DEALING WITH ANGER

My anger gave me the impetus to begin writing letters in my journal, and doing so helped me the most during this stage of grieving.

I especially enjoyed writing angry letters to God. With anger at others, I would sometimes feel guilty, but my feeling was God could take it. Here is an example of one of them:

Dear God,
I thought you were on my side. How could you do this to me? I used to think you were a punishing God, but I had decided

you were loving and kind. This is so mean. Why would you take Bob when we were just working everything out? He was so happy to be a new therapist, and we were learning to help each other and get along better. Why would you interrupt all that?

Are you punishing me? I thought you were better than that and that life could be fair. You don't make any sense. I am so mad at you for taking him from me.

Go fuck yourself.

Susan

Here is another letter I wrote shortly after Chris died, while I was in the throes of my initial grieving:

Dear God,

I was afraid you would take Chris away, but I never really thought you would. I always thought you would help her get better. I see so many people recover all the time. Why not her? I could see how my sweet girl would have been, and she even was for a time. She was so special. I thought you would spare her, and me.

I feel so punished. I know I messed up with her—I was so stoned when she was a teen, not even knowing she'd been sexually abused by a male friend I trusted. I hate you for taking my daughter. Maybe I deserved to lose her because of my addiction, but I don't really think so. You are punishing me and I hate you for it. I'm afraid of you again. I thought I was through that. I can't live without her. You know how much I loved her. I am angry and afraid and afraid of how angry I am.

Susan

I had to be ruthless, and I was.

Those letters were hard to live with after I wrote them, but I felt some immediate relief while I wrote. The ones about Chris were so childlike and raw. My journal contained many of my feelings, and I used it almost every day. Gradually I would come to accept that life doesn't always make sense and is often not "fair," but at that time, I just learned to let my anger out in safe ways.

Pause. Take Three Breaths. Consider: How much or how little do you blame God for this loss? Do you blame the person who died? Is there any way you are blaming yourself for this loss? The objects of our anger do change, so those answers will be different at any given time, but there are patterns to our anger. And we need to give ourselves permission to feel it and to let it move through us.

Give yourself permission for your anger to go wherever you need it to. At times I wanted to tell everyone to go fuck themselves, especially people who were not in loss the way I was. I didn't do that, and I don't recommend it. My journal was my companion and held all my wrath.

I also did a lot of emotional work at the ocean while I walked on the beach. Someone suggested throwing rocks or shells into the ocean, so I would stand at the shore and throw rocks in the ocean as hard as I could. Sometimes I would yell if no one was around. I have always connected with the ocean because of the feeling I get from being near it, near the powerful Spirit of the world and the essential mystery of life. So throwing something at it made me feel both powerful and powerless at the same time—just what grieving feels like. In one sense, you are whistling in the wind, and in another, you are a force to be reckoned with.

Another anger release technique I used was tearing paper. I had always enjoyed ripping up papers while I was paying bills and doing paperwork. When someone close dies, there is often a lot of paperwork to do. Bob was pretty organized, but there were still papers on and in his desk. I went through them early on to sort out his life insurances. I remember sitting at his desk, ripping up his old papers into little pieces—sometimes crying, sometimes not.

When Chris died, there was very little paperwork. She had been in rehab and then homeless for at least a year. I do remember ripping up some files with her old rehab bills. The files were thick and took a lot of effort to rip when I was feeling so weak. However, I mustered the energy for it, and it gave me a slight relief. I also remember having her autopsy report on my desk and then ripping it up in a moment of rage after I read she was six weeks pregnant at the time of her death.

With that news from the coroner's report, my anger erupted. I had to face the anger I'd had toward Chris about bearing two little babies without any preparation for parenthood. I had had to protect both little girls from their mother's addiction, and had taken painful legal action to get custody of Kaya until her father was ready to take over. Although I loved both of my granddaughters Kaya and China, from the moment they were born, I felt very angry about Chris's irresponsibility and the pain she had caused those two innocent girls—and me as well.

Then I had to face my own lack of preparation for motherhood. At twenty-five, I was such an immature and ambivalent mother, ill-prepared for the responsibilities of parenting. That's when my anger turned toward me.

Pinning It on Myself

I had no problem "siding with myself" about Bob's death and had no blame for myself for his passing. There was some slight regret about not pursuing the doctors more, but Bob was in charge of his own medical care, and I didn't take responsibility for any mistakes that were made. I regretted hurting him at times in occasional arguments, but there was no blame for his death.

However, with Chris I did blame myself for her death—deeply and often. I was an addicted mother, dependent on marijuana from the time my kids were preteens until they were sixteen and seventeen years old. Then my daughter died of addiction. I totally blamed myself for the negative role model I had been and the neglect and damage I had done as a chemically altered mother. I was furious with myself and needed every minute of my sixteen years of recovery to get through it. I felt the self-hatred returning, and I had to deal with it.

I dealt with my self-hatred mostly by sharing about it. My support system was very comforting to me and often had to help me through self-blame. "You did not kill your daughter, heroin did. She had the same illness of addiction that you had. It's not your fault," were statements I could not hear too often during the first months of my grief for Chris.

Relationship Problems as a Result of Anger from Loss

We all know of families that have fallen apart after a death, including parents, siblings, or other family members who never spoke to each other again. The sources for angry conflict are almost limitless, but the most typical are money and inheritance. Others can range from who speaks at the funeral to who took more care of the deceased when he or she was alive, and many other significant and insignificant details.

I always thought Chris would get sober, but when that door of hope closed for the last time, I felt crushed and hopeless. I also felt punished because my parenting had been so flawed and immature. I was like a kid raising kids, and I'd done a lot of damage, especially during the prolonged divorce.

As I've written, my ex-husband, Ed, was the favorite target for my anger. And I think I was also his. This was very true when Chris died, but I was even mad at him during Bob's illness and death. We tend to have habitual targets for our anger, which sometimes makes no sense at all.

Ed certainly didn't deserve my wrath when Bob died, but it

didn't matter; the feelings were there. I was angry with Ed for still being alive when Bob was gone. And I was sometimes angry with myself, too. I could give myself permission to be alive, but "It's okay that I am alive and they are not" gave me trouble. It often does not feel okay that certain people are alive and your loved one is not. I was angry with Ed for still being alive when Bob was gone. These are the kinds of angry reactions that are part of the process of loss. It is a time to ruthlessly give yourself permission to feel whatever you feel.

My ex-husband had good reason to feel anger with me. After I left the marriage, when our kids were ten and eleven years old, I went into a very rebellious period of smoking pot daily and behaving like I was a teenager. I had been the stable one in our marriage, and Ed had trusted me to take care of our children when we were separated. Their basic needs were met, but I became more like a friend to them than a stable mother. Ed only found out about that when Chris was thirteen and started to have her own substance abuse problems. I know he was shocked.

After Chris went into treatment, Ed and I worked hard on having a healed divorce. We did lots of family therapy, off and on, for years. I took responsibility for my own addiction to marijuana and was sober from the time Chris was sixteen. Ed forgave me for the damage I had done. I still have a photograph of a bouquet of roses that the family therapist had him send me one Mother's Day with a card about how he knew I'd been a decent mother to our children. We had done a lot of work toward forgiving each other.

At the time of Chris's death, we were still trying to cooperate over her last rehab experience. From the time China was four until her mother's death, we did many family sessions and kept in touch with each other about sharing the responsibility for our granddaughter's care. (Her older sister Kaya lived with her father during that time). However, after Chris died there was an explosion of anger between us, and we couldn't communicate at all. We blamed each other for our daughter's death. Despite all the work we had done, the anger returned and dominated our relationship.

This is a delicate area where behaving ruthlessly can do permanent damage. The anger response to loss explains how many relationships are disrupted by a death in the family. This is even true of healthy families.

Healthy versus Unhealthy Outlets for Anger

You can be ruthless in your journal and ask others, "How dare you . . ." but in real life, you do have to be careful. Ask for counsel from someone you trust when you're angry at your mother-in-law for usurping your role at the funeral, or at your brother for receiving a larger inheritance. Conflict is a reason to reach out for help because your judgment might be off. At the same time, you may need to assert some of your perceptions and wishes. Talking to someone you trust can help you with "the wisdom to know the difference." Beware and be aware of demonizing anyone in your life after a loss. In your mind's eye you will want to do that and probably will for a time. Just know it is a part of your grief process, and use some healthy judgment about who you tell about it.

My journal is filled with angry letters to Ed. I really let it rip. Sometimes I would hit on a phrase I felt I could tell him; for example, "I'm sorry I made so many mistakes with our daughter. I know you made some, too. Let's not continue the damage with our grandchildren." We were just not able to get on the same wavelength enough to make a healed divorce possible. To this day, I envy couples who have healed divorces. I have not yet accomplished that in my lifetime.

After Chris died, I saw the film *In the Bedroom*. It was about a family who lost a son to addiction and murder. There was a tremendous amount of conflict between the parents and his girlfriend after he died. What was most interesting to me was that the parents seemed to have had a good marriage. There were scenes of affection and connection before their son died suddenly. However, as their grief unfolded, their needs and styles of grieving were so different that it caused a tremendous disruption in their marriage. The father wanted to spend time with his son's girlfriend because she had been close to him and loved him, but the mother couldn't face her at all and was angry with her.

The father wound up murdering the man who had killed their son in some dealings with drugs.

It is natural to want to seek revenge against anyone who you feel has caused your loss. Don't physically harm anyone, no matter how much you may want to. I have murdered people in my mind, but thankfully have had enough impulse control not to carry it out. Remember, that was a movie—do not turn to violence. But violent wishes? Yes. I encourage you to allow yourself to have angry—even violent—fantasies, but to also be aware of becoming too destructive in your own mind and of not getting stuck in them in unhealthy ways. All our emotions move through us. With anger, it is particularly important to allow the flow of angry energy without becoming destructive to ourselves or others.

The movie showed me that the death of a child could destroy even the healthiest relationships. This helped me understand what happened in my relationship with Ed.

A tremendous amount of conflict can erupt after a death in the family. I mentioned earlier the conflict my brother and I had when our mother was dying. We both believed we were doing most of the work for her. Fortunately, we had a family therapy session in which we vented our frustrations, and the therapist was able to translate our respective situations to each other. We have been quite close since then. My brother says it helped because I finally understood his position, but I know it helped him understand me, as well.

My friend James tells the story about his brother and him standing at his mother's deathbed. His mother whispered in his ear,

"Don't fight with your brother, Jimmy." He responded to her, "Tell him." He says she smiled, knowing he was kidding and not kidding at the same time. Anger and hostility in families does not just go away because someone is dying or has died.

I know of many families in which the conflict over inheritance and who got what has caused permanent rifts and years of bad feelings. Sometimes all hell breaks loose when the family matriarch or patriarch dies. Often a powerful matriarch or patriarch has kept a lid on deep conflicts in the family and enforced positive behavior. When they die, all bets are off and the conflicts can emerge full force. When people are unaware of the anger and rage that can get triggered, they tend to act it out on those around them. Be careful.

Pause. Take Three Breaths. Consider: How have your friendships or family relationships been since your loss? Have any conflicts arisen, or has anything erupted since this death? Are you aware of any distortions in your perception of the conflict? Are there any healing actions you might take to improve the situation or protect your future connections?

There's a fine line between giving ourselves permission to have feelings including anger and rage, and doing permanent damage to relationships we might want to maintain. Some people who have not been in touch with anger in their lives in general, or who have been mostly shut down emotionally, can have extra challenges from the anger that comes up as part of grieving.

Unresolved Grief and Anger

Unfinished or incomplete grief from losses tends to emerge when we experience another loss; this is called transference. We tend to transfer any unresolved feelings toward people from our history onto the current situation. One loss brings up all other losses.

Writing letters not sent can help with this. I would write an angry letter to Ed and then realize I would have loved to have said some of the same things to my father. "Dear Ex" moves to "Dear Dad" quite easily, when you are aware of it. It's helpful when you can make some of those deep, emotional connections with what you are feeling in your mourning. This is how the grief process can eventually help you become more whole.

The anger phase of grief is where a lot of people get stuck. If you are uncomfortable with anger and are used to denying it, you may have difficulty moving on. A good example can be found in the fourth season of the television show *Downton Abbey*. The eldest daughter of the family, Mary, loses her husband suddenly in a car crash. She has just given birth to their first child. She is so bitter that she even has difficulty bonding with her newborn son. Responding to many comments made to her by loving friends and family, she simply says, "My husband is dead." "But what about the baby?" they ask her, to which she responds, "My husband is dead."

Of course, this is a TV show, but it is a good example of the process of grieving. We often need to stay with the dead for a while, and we need permission to do that. Again, only you can give yourself that permission. Eventually you'll need to give yourself permission to rejoin the living, which takes time, and being pushed doesn't help. Someone attuned to your grieving process can help to guide you, but cannot take the lead.

I saw a woman who had seemed to handle the loss of her son in a plane crash in a healthy and graceful way. A few months after her seeming recovery, she got very depressed. When she came to see me, she confessed she had been boiling inside. She had thought she should remain strong for the rest of her family, but she was in a rage. She could not forgive her son for getting into that private plane with a family member who he'd been told was an unsafe pilot. In a couple of therapy sessions, I was able to help her express the anger she had been holding back so she could move forward in her grief.

Living with unresolved feelings can be torturous. We often need someone else to help us express what feels like the most unacceptable parts of our grief. Ruthlessness helps a lot. "This is how I feel, and no one can tell me not to feel this" is another permission you can give yourself.

Choosing the Living

When you have feelings that are hard to understand or don't make sense, give yourself permission to have them. It is okay to say, "Of course I'm angry." I encourage you to accept your anger in a way you may never have before. You're alive, and anger is a part of living. If you're alive, you will experience anger. And if you've experienced the loss of someone close, of course you're angry.

When the character of Mary in *Downton Abbey* mourns to the point where she isn't able to function, she is told by the head servant, "You have been remaining with the dead. It's time to return to the living." My "return to the living" began by spending time with my son and with Chris's two daughters.

Pause. Take Three Breaths. Consider: Are there any letters you need to write (but not send) to anyone or anything you are continually angry with? Are there any actions you need to take to begin your "return to the living"?

THINGS TO REMEMBER

- Anger and even rage are parts of grieving.

- Anger is not rational and emerges in many different ways. It doesn't have to make sense.

- Anger wants to blame and will blame anyone: the deceased, yourself, doctors, family members, even God.

- Letters to the deceased, to people in your life (often not sent), and to God can help you through your anger.

- Anger-releasing techniques can help to vent the anger, and they do no harm to anyone. Keeping a journal can be essential to expressing and containing feelings of anger, grief, and loss.

- Connecting with nature, like spending time by water, is helpful.

- Find small stress-releasing techniques, such as ripping paper.

- Anger and the different styles of grieving can disrupt relationships. This needs care and attention and possibly some reaching out for help.

- The angry phase of grief is where a lot of people get stuck. Don't hesitate to vent in safe ways that hopefully do no harm.

- Be expressive, but do it with care.

- As you work your way through the anger of grieving, notice moments of choosing life.

CHAPTER 6

Obsessions: What-Ifs, Regrets, and Resentments

I have always loved Édith Piaf's song, "Non, Je Ne Regrette Rien" (No, I Regret Nothing). Regretting nothing is a bold way to approach life, and, in my experience, that state of mind is pretty hard to come by. Twelve-Step programs offer a related promise: "We will not regret the past nor wish to shut the door on it," a bold promise to which I do not totally relate. We are bound to regret some aspects of what we had with our loved ones after they are gone.

For me, the most challenging regrets to give up have been the terrible mistakes I made with my children. Before I could do that, however, I needed to know what those mistakes were and to feel them and express them. I also had to review in my mind's eye every part of the relationships and what I experienced with my children, positive and negative.

I want to share this with you, not to be confessional or self-flagellating, but to tell you about being a flawed human, about all of us being grieving, flawed humans. I had so many more regrets about how I had been with Chris, as her mother, than I ever had about Bob. But I had regrets about how I treated him at times, as well. Your situations and relationships are probably very different from mine, but the human imperfections and how you feel about your faults after a loved one is gone are a big part of the challenges of grief.

Remember, we are heading toward acceptance—acceptance of them, acceptance of them being gone, acceptance of ourselves, and acceptance of the relationship in all its many facets. This is a tall order, and it takes as long as it takes. In the meantime, you need to process the relationship and all the aspects of how you each were in it, including going through any regrets or disappointments in yourself and in the other person. You also have to process how he or she died and your feelings about what happened to them in their dying process. Hence the need for ruthlessness and lots of permissions.

Pause. Take Three Breaths. Consider: How much or how little have you been thinking about them? Give yourself full permission to think and talk about them as much as you want.

OBSESSING

In the process of grieving, there is a great deal of reworking and mentally reliving your history with loved ones. Your thoughts tend to be consumed with those who have died, and with your experiences with them and your feelings toward them, both positive and negative. There can be a tendency to idealize them after they are gone, for them to become "sainted." It's wonderful to remember how great they were (if they were that to you), but beware of unfounded positivity. It is important to be as honest and realistic as you can as you process this loss and your relationship to the person who has died. This is another ruthless demand on your proactive approach to grieving.

There are usually regrets, and sometimes, major feelings of guilt or even shame, in a close loss. I thought a lot about my marriage to Bob and what I might have done differently, especially wishing I had

105

appreciated him more. When Chris died, I obsessed about what a bad mother I'd been and all the mistakes I had made with both of my children as they were growing up. I also would remember the good times with both of them and shed some tears. Permission to go through the history, positive and negative, and all the feelings involved, and permission to think about them all the time is key to proceeding with your grief.

Until I was dealing with the deaths of two people I deeply loved, I never realized that what Elisabeth Kübler-Ross calls the *bargaining stage* is so extremely obsessive. You will probably be obsessed with the person who has died and your history with him or her for quite some time. That's not all negative, but my thoughts often went to wishing I had been more loving and appreciative of my dear husband and daughter. I found I had to process every part of my relationship with both Bob and Chris, and processing occupied a lot of my thinking and feelings for many months.

Pause. Take Three Breaths. Consider: Have you been obsessed with your loved ones since they died? Do you think of them often? Do you think about them most of the time with regrets or resentments? With appreciation? Can you give yourself permission to be obsessed with them right now?

WHAT-IFS

I had so many regrets about how I was during Chris's addiction I could not count them. I couldn't help entertaining many thoughts about how things might have been if I had behaved differently. Early on, when I was addicted to marijuana myself, I didn't have a chance at being an effective parent. When Chris was sixteen and Bill was seventeen, I went into recovery and did not do drugs or drink from that time on. Of course I regretted not going into recovery sooner. What if I'd been sober from the time they were born? What if I'd been teachable during all my training and taken it in on a personal basis, instead of living in my head most of the time while I was getting my Ph.D. in psychology?

After I got sober and went into recovery, I was still quite lost. I had to face how I had not been present with my son, as well as my dead daughter. I was extremely unattuned to Bill's needs throughout his childhood. Bill always responded to help and was easier to deal with than Chris. Later, when the problems in our family came to the surface, counselors would tell Bill what to do to get better, and he would mostly just do it. He was essentially a healthy kid who grew up to be a fabulous adult.

I would obsess about how Chris, with her highly rebellious spirit, was so much more of a challenge for me. She would not conform. What if I'd been more capable of guiding or disciplining her? I would get frustrated, and I'd just collapse and let her do what she wanted. Early in my recovery I learned that when the parents can't agree, it puts the kids in charge of the household. That is what happened with our family, and I had to relook at all of it. What if I had been healthier and more conscious earlier on and not been addicted? And on and on and on. . . .

Eventually I had to find the ruthless part of me so that I could learn to have compassion for myself and decide to stop the obsessive self-hatred and self-recrimination. How can you live with yourself when you've made so many serious mistakes with your kids, and one of them has died? The concept I had developed of "side with yourself" became helpful over time, but there were torturous moments of regret, self-hatred, and self-doubt. It took at least a year after Chris's death to come to the compassion of being on my own side most of the time.

So give yourself permission to obsess about your deceased loved ones and your relationships with them as much as you need to. In going over and over this, you are working it out. Know that you might have bouts of self-hatred or, at the very least, self-doubt about things you did and didn't do while they were alive. Remember to write about it as much as you need to.

Pause. Take Three Breaths. Consider: What are some of the "what-ifs" that haunted you after your loved one died? Are some of them still with you? What are they? Write them down.

REGRETS

The most predominant form my obsessions took was in regrets. I had many regrets about how I'd been with Bob, even though we'd had what I considered a good marriage. In hindsight, I felt there were major ways I'd been quite selfish with my second husband.

I realized how much I had measured what I was doing for him compared with what he was doing for me. This measuring of who was doing more in the marriage was most apparent in the kitchen. We had an agreement that whoever cooked did not have to clean up. We had quite a few arguments about that: "I did most of the cooking tonight, and you're not doing most of the cleanup." I started to realize what a waste of time this kind of discussion was when Bob was so ill. I found that I had to do most of everything, and it was fine. It was so much easier than maintaining that measuring attitude. After he died, I regretted our arguments even more.

My regrets about Bob were predominantly about my attitude toward him. Many times I wouldn't express my frustration, but it was in me. I'd think, "Look how much he talks about cooking, and I still do most of the cooking," and after his death I came to regret that resentful attitude. I wished I had been more generous in my spirit toward him and our marriage. A lot of measuring had happened in my own mind, but I regretted letting it color too much of our domestic experience.

I had many regrets around Bob's illness. What if I had been a healthier cook? What if we hadn't eaten sugar together? What if I had helped him more after he developed diabetes? What if I had encouraged him more about doctoring and checkups? What if I had encouraged him to go for the scans right after the surgery and hadn't trusted the doctors when they said they "got it all"? Questioning everything in my mind seemed like an endless process.

I know there were some people around me who felt that Bob and I hadn't handled all the medical decisions well. My son, Bill, didn't understand why we hadn't had Bob's brain and bones checked earlier. None of his doctors had suggested it, but we could have been more proactive in exploring his health options. His kidney surgery was in the spring, and in the fall we found out the cancer had spread to both bone and brain. By then, it was too late for any effective treatment. Bob did radiation for six weeks, but the oncologist told us kidney cancer often "spits" at treatment of any kind.

I questioned the whole medical process after he died and in hindsight, I regretted some of our decisions. Sometimes I would look back and see some of the signs of his cancer, like his substantial weight loss (about which he was very proud). I wished we had looked into everything earlier and been more aware. After going back and forth about it in my mind for months, I came to realize Bob and I had had the best summer of our lives that year. If we had been visiting doctors all summer, it would have been a very different time. We were both so happy to be alive, feeling like he had beaten the cancer. We had a beautiful and grateful summer. Those thoughts helped to eventually move me toward acceptance of what had happened in the course of Bob's illness.

The obsessions with what happened with Chris were filled with much deeper regrets, mostly because I had made so many serious mistakes with my children growing up. After witnessing and being a part of Chris's horrifying decline into heroin addiction, it was difficult to remember the good times. I did eventually remember the joyful moments, but those memories were mixed with the mistakes I'd made as an extremely ambivalent mother. Having been in a highly

109

conflicted marriage, the joy of raising two children was tainted, at best. After Chris died I looked through lots of pictures of our first little family. William and Christie (their childhood names) were sixteen months apart.

Most of the years of my first marriage felt like an emergency, with Ed's endless medical training, moving all around the country, and trying to write a Ph.D. dissertation while having babies. Because of that, it was mostly in hindsight that I could appreciate having had two healthy, beautiful children who were both very spirited and curious and playful and so much fun. If only I could have relaxed and enjoyed that time more. I sorely wished I could have appreciated what I had with them, especially when I was grieving my deceased daughter.

In my grief, I deeply regretted not being ready to mother them. I remembered how adorable they were, two little blond babies full of life and love, and wishing I had appreciated having them when I did. Because they were so close in age, I often thought of them as "the kids" and wished I had treated them more as individuals. What if I'd had them later or not had them so close together? I knew my thinking wasn't making a lot of sense, but I couldn't help needing to go through every part of my life with them. I'd remember Cub Scouts and Brownies and making Christmas tree ornaments with them. We made painted wooden ones, fake stained glass, Mexican "Eyes of God" with yarn, and one year, even sewn candy canes. I still have a few of those ornaments, and Bill puts them on his family's tree at Christmas.

Pause. Take Three Breaths. Consider: How much did you appreciate your loved one when he or she was alive? How much can you appreciate him or her now? See if you can remember all the things you do appreciate about what you had with your loved one. You will almost certainly feel like you didn't have enough appreciation for him or her. I suggest you write some of these thoughts in your journal.

I even wished for a while that I had stayed with their father. We were extremely incompatible, but in my grief I thought I should have stayed because it might have saved my daughter's life. Every family I saw looked so much more stable than ours—and mostly, they were. If I'd worked less, cooked more, had more dinners at home, moved out but stayed in the Westchester area near their father, rather than fleeing to Long Island in an impulsive way, maybe Chris would have lived. These were the thoughts of someone obsessed about the "what ifs."

A friend had said I could move in with her and her daughter with my kids, and within weeks I'd done it. I took my kids out of school in November. Who does that? One of my deepest regrets was not protecting my children from the pain of the divorce. I'd seen and even helped people to not include their children in the inherent conflicts during a divorce. However, when my children were young teenagers, I treated them more like friends. This was partly because I was smoking a lot of marijuana at the time, and partly because I was just immature and had bad boundaries with my children. I was not mature enough to be the mother who contained a lot of her thoughts and feelings when it came to her offspring or protected them from adult issues and responsibilities. And I certainly could not do that stoned.

After Chris's death, I was filled with self-recrimination and self-hatred. "I should have stayed," "I should have left in a better way," "I should have just sucked it up and given up my life for my kids," "I should have never smoked so much marijuana," "I should never have smoked pot with Bill and Chris when they were so young." Each thought had truth in it, except for the ones in which I felt that I had killed my daughter. Those thoughts about having killed her still come to me at times, but I can face the truth in them, face my very flawed mothering, and know I am still a good person.

Pause. Take Three Breaths. Consider: Do you have regrets about anything in your relationships with your loved ones? What are some of the things you regret about how you were with them? About how they were with you? About how they died? Consider writing some of this out in your journal.

Appreciation and Positive "Regrets"

The regrets are not all completely negative. In my experience with the loss of Bob and Chris, after I finished clubbing myself with self-recriminations, I began to remember more of the positive parts of the relationship and regretted not appreciating them or enjoying them more. These were more melancholy moments as I remembered the good times.

With Bob, I just wished I had appreciated him more. He was very independent. He took care of himself in lots of ways I had taken for granted. He had decided to go to graduate school for social work early in our marriage, and did it seamlessly in three years without interrupting much of our life together. He would take his own time to write a paper or take a class, never complaining much about the work, and he really enjoyed it and enjoyed sharing it with me. I loved that he was doing it and doing it so well.

We then shared a profession—being psychotherapists—for about five years. I would refer people to him, and we would discuss challenging cases in interesting and creative ways. Bob was extremely compassionate and a natural at therapy. He had also done over ten years of his own therapy and recovery process. After being an actor for thirty years, he had found a second career he deeply enjoyed, and he loved sharing it with me. I just wish I had appreciated more what we had together while we still had each other close.

Bob was a family man who had not been able to have children in his first marriage. There was not a question of us having any, since I was in my late forties when we met, but we wound up having two grandchildren together, and Bob was thrilled. Our first, Kaya, was born in our house with a midwife, and we were both very close to Kaya and involved in her life from the beginning. Chris was in and out of her addiction, so we became surrogate parents for stretches of time in Kaya's early life. Sometimes we joked that we "had to get married" for the grandchildren.

We thoroughly enjoyed Kaya and then China, who arrived four years later. However, since Chris was an addict and sinking into a heroin addiction by the time China was one, it put the burden of their care on us for extended periods of time. I never appreciated how hard that must have been on Bob and how great he was about it. In fact, at the time, I had the opposite feelings and resented him for his resistance to us getting more involved.

Bob had a very challenging relationship with my daughter, and I had wished he'd been more involved with her. But Chris was oppositional, and how could he not have had his own pain about that? Bob came from an addicted family as well, with two sisters who died of their addictions. I knew it was painful for him to see Chris's deterioration, especially as it affected me and our two beloved granddaughters. Bob would lock horns with Chris over her outrageous behavior, and I would sometimes feel torn.

I had sometimes blamed Bob for us not taking Chris in or for not taking more responsibility for the girls. In fact, we had taken on plenty, and he was so loving about the whole process, considering the challenges of having little girls dropped into our lives at random moments and sometimes staying for months at a time. We had so many mixed feelings about Chris and her two girls that we would sometimes fight about it.

Once he was gone, I regretted not being more on his side and appreciating all the sacrifices he'd made to be a responsible husband and grandfather. Then when Chris died, I felt the tangled relationship they'd had was now tangled up in death. I was tangled too, and I needed to make time to grieve them separately and together. I had one photograph of them together taken two years before they died that I kept out in my bedroom with a candle, and I pictured them together on the Other Side.

RESENTMENT

After I left my first marriage, I came to realize how much I still tended to be resentful of my partner, no matter what he was doing. I had found during my recovery process that I was fueled by resentment toward my first husband. Of course, there were some good reasons to have resentment in my alcoholic marriage, but feeling resentful had become a way of life for me. It was how I experienced the world a lot of the time in my early, married life. If a friend asked, "Would you like to go to a concert?" my response would be, "He would never go." In the course of the divorce and my own recovery, I had realized how much I referenced my partner in any of my decisions or thoughts about myself. I had done a lot of emotional work during my marriage to Bob to become more aware of and focused on my own experience.

However, after Bob died, I had to face the fact that I had persisted in my tendency to resent who I was with, regardless of his actions. There were remnants of my old resentments from my first marriage. Although I had been working on some of those while Bob and I were married, I had to face that habit of mine more deeply after Bob died.

Resenting him didn't have to totally make sense. My resentment was really a desire that I should have been able to do something to keep him alive. I was desperately looking for something to explain this horrible loss and things I might have done to prevent it. It had to make sense, and often the only sense I could make of it was that it was my fault or someone else's. I eventually had to come to terms with my powerlessness in these situations and that I could not control when and how my loved ones died.

When Chris died, my resentments transferred mostly to my ex-husband. I had gone through a prolonged divorce of three years and blamed him for most of it. In hindsight, I now see I was an equal part in the whole process and very often even more responsible for the debacle of our marriage. However, in my grief, I regressed to my old resentments and had to go through much of my old anger for some time.

There were also times when I found myself resenting Chris for succumbing to her addictive illness, when so many people do recover and come back to their families and to their children. I resented her for abandoning my two beloved granddaughters. I felt that especially when I would see them suffering from being motherless girls. I did resent people who had living, grown daughters, and sometimes I would put the blame for that on her. Mostly, I blamed Ed or myself. I was still recovering from being fueled by resentment in my earlier life, and my grief caused me to regress back into it frequently.

Pause. Take Three Breaths. Consider: Are you someone who tends to carry resentments? Do you resent your loved one for dying? Do you resent anything about how he or she was in the relationship with you? Is there anyone else you resent in your life right now? Consider writing some of this down as well.

WRITE IT OUT

Writing down your obsessive thoughts is a wonderful way to break the endless loop of repetitive thinking. Remember to use your journal. A blank book can be a companion for you, and one of the most useful tools for exploring your obsessive thoughts, owning them, and interrupting that pattern of thinking. Your journal can contain so much of your grief and eventually free you from some of the suffering involved in loss.

Many people resist writing their grief. Writing does bring up feelings, and it can be painful. A new client of mine who lost his son a few months ago to addiction finally reported he had written a few pages. He said he had to stop a few times because it was painful and he was crying. Then he paused and said, "I guess that's the point." This is part of the ruthlessness of grief. You will need to face the pain in order to go through it. Journal writing helps you to be ruthless on your own behalf and to face what is happening on the deepest level of going through loss.

I recently read a book about writing out your grief, titled *Braving the Fire*. The title reflects the courage it takes to be proactive after loss by keeping a journal of your grief. It is counterintuitive to go into the fire, but in my experience it is the only healthy way to safety and health.

I would write on and on about the things I might have done differently. I am modeling a lot of that here in this book. I encourage you to write your own and know that it can help you. Just put down the narrative of your inner life and see what happens.

Letters not sent can also be very important to this part of your process. For example, I would write to my ex-husband about my anger or things I had been obsessing about that I wished he had done differently. Then I would usually feel some anger or sadness, and then the feelings would pass. Sometimes I would write the letters on separate paper and rip them up into little pieces. At other times I would put them in my journal and just keep them there.

The most powerful letter writing turned out to be writing to the ones I had lost. For example, I wrote, "Dear Chris, Words cannot express how sorry I am for failing to be there when you needed me." These letters allowed me to imagine owning my mistakes and imagine her hearing my amends. Before she died, and after I had been in my own recovery for a while, whenever I would actually try to apologize to her she would always deny she had any problems with the careless and sometimes destructive mothering I had given her. The letters to her after she was gone allowed me to complete some communication with her and also deal with my deep regrets and imagine she could finally hear me.

I found writing letters to myself and to my former self were helpful. I would pick an age when I'd made some of my worst mistakes and write to myself about them. I could be angry or compassionate by turns, but I needed to get the feelings out.

Dear Susan at age 37,

You were so lost, and you thought you were such a great mother. I know you didn't realize what you were doing, but you should have. You decided to move out of Bronxville with no real plan for the future of your children or yourself. If only you had thought about it more. You were so desperate to leave the marriage that you forgot about how it would affect them. If only you could have waited until you had a better plan. Moving in with your friend on Long Island was a pipe dream, and you just did it. If only you had considered the children's feelings more. I wish you had gotten an apartment and not yanked them out of school at ages ten and eleven and made them leave everything they knew at such a tender age. Chris was especially sensitive, and I remember how she didn't show when she was hurt.

And if only you had protected Chris from some of the people you were around in your own addiction. She might not have been sexually abused. What if you were more protective of her and careful of what you put her through? She might be alive today.

Coming to terms with the damage I had done in my addicted mothering required ruthless grieving. Write your grief out, face the fire, and be proactive in dealing with whatever your history and feelings with your lost loved one have been. What we resist persists, and we ultimately want to complete this grieving process.

TALK IT OUT

Feel free to talk about your loved one as much as you want or need to. I told one recovery group I frequented that the group was going to hear about Chris and Bob until I was done talking about them, and eventually I (mostly) was. I think a lot of people get stuck in worrying about what other people think of their process or that people don't want to hear about their loss anymore. This is another place for ruthless grieving. Give yourself as much time as you need. Your listeners will tell you when it's enough, and then you'll find someone else to talk with about your loved ones—and that's fine.

It's very helpful to talk about the person who died with someone else who loved him or her, too. I talked a lot with Bill about Chris. Because he was her brother, we had so much shared history with her. I was careful to protect him from some of my deepest obsessions and regrets, but we spoke about her often, and I think it helped us both. I spoke a lot to Kaya and China about their mother, and I know it helped us all. "Your mother would be so happy about this," or "She loved doing this with you" was music to all our ears.

I spoke a lot to Bob's friends and family about him. I would call them specifically to speak about him. His cousin Sandy and I spent a lot of time together, mostly talking about Bob and remembering him with love, tears, and even humor. It's a wonderful mutuality because others need to talk about their loss, too. Talk to people you trust about any doubts you have about how you were with your loved one. They probably knew your relationship. Sometimes it would mean the world to me to hear people tell me I was good with Bob or Chris, or how much they had cared about me.

Pause. Take Three Breaths. Consider: Are you talking about your loved one as much as you still want to? Are you afraid you speak about him or her too much? Who are your favorite people to talk to about the person you lost? Could you give yourself permission to speak about him or her as much as you need to?

The obsessive phase blends into the pure sadness and depression of grief as the past gets worked through in going over all the possibilities, the "What ifs." The positive, loving aspects of the relationship usually become even stronger, and the depth of the pure sadness emerges full force. It just feels so sad that they are gone and not coming back.

If I could get through my painful history, you can get through yours.

THINGS TO REMEMBER

- You will be thinking constantly—even obsessing—about the person who has died for many months and probably at least a year.

- There are bound to be some regrets, even resentments, in every human relationship. Let yourself feel them, and tell someone about them, too.

- Give yourself permission to think about all the wonderful parts of your relationship as well as the negatives.

- Use your journal for all the "What-ifs." It's helpful to get your feelings out and to see your story written out.

- Letters not sent or to the deceased can help with your obsessing about your loved one and about specific issues you had with anyone about this loss.

- Talk about your loved one and your relationship with him or her as much as you need to. Don't decide it is enough until you are complete with the process. Especially speak with people who loved the person who died. It's a beautiful mutuality. They need to talk about their loss, too.

CHAPTER 7

Sadness and Depression: Allowing Your Depth

Of course you have been feeling sad throughout your mourning. But after you've wrestled your mind to the ground, there is a deep, abiding sadness you will probably have to allow. Let yourself go there. It's one of the paradoxes of grief—and a ruthless part, as well—that the sadness does not diminish as we progress in the first year but actually seems to broaden and deepen. I suggest you let it.

Sadness and depression can make us feel very lost and even afraid. The fear often comes from not feeling safe in the world. We tend to think, "If this loss could happen, then anything could happen," and that thought isn't pretty. The entire process of grief requires us to allow for feelings that we may have always had difficulty allowing. And we need to find ways to feel safe enough to allow them. Even more than anger and guilt, I think I was the most challenged by needing to allow myself to just feel so sad.

FEELING (SORRY) FOR YOURSELF

Conditioning has taught us to not allow for simple sadness in our lives. Sometimes people will think—and even say aloud—"You are just feeling sorry for yourself." Of course you're feeling sorry for yourself. You've lost someone who was close to you. Rather than labeling it as *feeling sorry for yourself*, I call it *feeling for yourself* or *having compassion for yourself.* I know you've been learning to do that in the course of your grief. Give yourself permission to feel sad and even depressed for a time. You will not always feel this way. Feelings change. Emotions move, as they have been moving through you since your loss. This is another opportunity to be ruthless about seeking out your negative thinking and working on shifting it when you can.

Sadness and depression are very different. Depression is characterized by a lack of movement of any kind. Sometimes we have to go there for a time. Sadness has more movement in it; although it is slow and even quiet, it moves.

In my family growing up, there was a definite emphasis on being cheerful. I think it was part of the American culture in the 40s and 50s after World War II. My father would often say to me, "Where's that smile?" He would say it especially if I was showing any anger or sadness. I hated him saying that to me, but didn't understand why until much later, when I realized I just wanted to be able to have my feelings and not have to be happy all the time.

Pause. Take Three Breaths. Consider: How are you at feeling for yourself? How are you at allowing yourself to feel sad? Are you able to cry when you feel it? How was your family with facing negative emotions like anger, fear, and sadness? What are some of the things you do when you feel sad? Consider writing some of this down in your journal.

DECISIONS IN SADNESS

The decisions I am talking about are internal decisions—not about selling your house or taking a trip, but about how your life might be or what life is about. I call them *depression decisions*. Make no decisions about life or about yourself when you are so sad. Don't make decisions about yourself, your loved one who is gone, life, or God.

122

The most common depression decision is, "I will always feel as bad as I do right now—it will never change." Others include, "I deserve to be this unhappy, I'm hopeless," "I didn't deserve to have that person in my life anyway," "I am being punished and don't deserve love in my life," "I don't want a new life—I want the old one or nothing at all." Of course these feelings come up, but no decisions should be made. Decisions made from your deepest sadness tend to be negative and can get you stuck in depression with no emotional movement of any kind. You might have these kinds of thoughts, but don't decide anything.

You might want to write out what your depression decisions tend to be. It's not that you won't have the tendency to think these thoughts, but it's helpful to be aware of them. You should also know that these thoughts are probably distortions and are the result of your loss, which is coloring all your thinking.

Pause. Take Three Breaths. Consider: Are you are making some internal decisions about life or yourself or your future that are colored by your sadness about this loss? Have you decided you can't go on? Have you decided you will always feel this way? Have you decided everything is hopeless? Have you decided you will never (or should never) be happy again? There is a big difference between having a thought and deciding it is true. What are some of your recurring thoughts that sound like decisions about life, or about yourself, or about the future? Just be aware that they are present.

EXPRESSIONS OF GRIEF

Experiencing the death of someone close shakes up all our ideas about life and the future and love and the stability of life. I like the text abbreviation that many young people use a lot to explain those feelings: WTF (which stands for *What the fuck*). I know this text abbreviation is overused, but it is never more apt than with a close death. It's easy to feel totally shaken to your core when you are in grief. If this can happen, what else could happen? This is also where fear creeps in. What will happen next?

Steven Levine writes, "Unattended sorrow is a stone stuck in the throat from 'swallowing our grief,' a boulder rolled into the entrance to the heart against our resurrection." We need to not swallow grief but to instead give it full expression. Pure sadness, as we are expressing it, takes our journey right into the depth of our hearts. While we are there, we can explore many aspects of ourselves and of life in a rich and meaningful way.

Knowing you'll never again see someone you love is just *so sad*. I couldn't believe I would never be in the presence of Bob or Chris ever again. After all the anger and regrets, the obsessing about them and the fears, I just cried and cried. I was so deeply sad.

I think this feeling is part of the origin of the religious belief that we will meet with our loved ones on "the Other Side." I am a spiritual person, but I'm not sure we get to see our loved ones again after we die. Whether or not you believe is up to you, but you do need to face that you will not see them again on this earth in the form you have known them. Sometimes you can feel them with you spiritually, even connect with them, but it is different from what you had, and there is no way around it: death is a loss on many levels.

Depth of Grief

There is actually no way to measure the depth of your sadness. It just is. Losing a child at any age takes us to our depth, where it seems we must remain for quite a long time. However, losing a partner or a parent can affect us as deeply as anything else. There is no comparing pain.

In Chapter 9, we will be taking a more thorough look at the part roles play in grieving. We will be examining the challenge to our identity that can arise from loss of various roles, including questions like, "Who am I if I'm not a mother?" that can threaten our very identity and deepen our pain.

For now, though, we are focusing on the pure sadness of grief and how to get through it. We need to feel it as fully as we can tolerate at any given moment, find ways to express it for as long as we need to, and then be open to new energy coming into our hearts.

Impermanence of Life

When Bob died, I deeply felt the impermanence of life. I thought about the Japanese monks who do sand paintings, meticulously making patterns with different colored sand. Then they perform the ritual of taking buckets and washing them away. It is a Buddhist spiritual practice that reminds us of the impermanence of life. That's exactly how I felt about my marriage with Bob: We had done a lot of work to build a healthy relationship and a full, rich life together, and then death came and washed it all away.

Of course, my grieving process was complicated by the loss of Chris so soon after Bob died. I was then even sadder. However, I was filled with such a mixture of emotions that the pure, deep sadness didn't come on for several months. That is often the way it is—you feel angry, you feel guilty, you obsess about your lost loved one like crazy, and then finally you just feel sad and, sometimes, depressed.

One of the saddest aspects of Bob's death at sixty-two was that his life and our lives together felt so interrupted. We had only eleven years together. Bob used to say that it felt like we'd been together for a century, but a short, quick century. I felt so sad that we didn't get more time together and didn't get to go as deep as I imagined we could have over time.

After he died, I prayed to Bob to help Chris. As I've said, I thought his death could save Chris somehow. I prayed so hard for him to help her that sometimes I felt like a total nag, and I could imagine or "hear" him telling me, "All right, I'm doing everything I can—relax." But then she died. I even felt angry with Bob and partially blamed him for her death, because I felt certain he could help with his "in" on the Other Side. Of course, he could not. Those ways of thinking were also a part of my deepest sadness. My feelings were all over the place. My bargaining mind was taking me everywhere and then I had to surrender to the fact that they were both gone and there was nothing I could do about it.

Pause. Take Three Breaths. Consider: How have you been about uncertainty in your life? How controlling do you think you are? How hard is it to face that there was nothing you could have done to prevent your loved one's death? I suggest you do some writing about it.

WAYS TO EXPRESS SADNESS

When I'm really feeling sad, I don't want to do much of anything, especially if it involves other people. I am often reminded of a Native American ritual where a mourner sits in a hole in the ground and is fed from above. Even writing in my journal felt like too much effort, but I had a strong desire to express my feelings, so I pushed through to write as much as I was able.

That sadness also feels very connected to love. I've heard people say that grief is love, that their tears for the person who died are filled with love. My friend Susan talks about how, for her, the deep pain of the sadness seemed to connect her with some joy in her heart. If grief is love, then, of course, there is joy in it—another paradox.

Initially I didn't want to do much of anything; I needed to just sit with my sad feelings, but as time moved on, I did have a strong desire to express my sadness in ways other than words. Someone told me about the practice of creating a mandala every day by making a circle and just filling the circle with colors in no particular design or order. I made those for a time, and it felt very good—no content, just pure feeling. I put the mandalas up around the house, and they felt nourishing and real.

Color can be a wonderful way to express our emotions. Sadness often feels especially wordless and more like the experience of color. We use the words "feeling blue" for sadness. Many aspects of sadness are truly beyond words.

Another way I expressed sadness was through collage. I used scraps of paper or the covers of some cards and photos from magazines or real pictures of us together, and then I pasted them to a paper background. I put them up in my bathroom, and they comforted me.

Pause. Take Three Breaths. Consider: Have you found tools to help you express your sadness? Can you be creative in finding a modality or action that would express it? Would you try some I've suggested? Making an altar or a scrapbook might help. Don't write about it. Do it.

Listening to Music

Music is another powerful way to express grief. Playing music your loved ones liked can be a beautiful way to connect with them and with all your feelings about them. Also remember to play your own favorite music, which can help you to connect with yourself, apart from other people, when you need that.

After Bob died, I listened to some of the chants we had played while he was so sick. Listening to them helped me shed my tears and just be with my feelings about my dear husband. However, I learned I had to be careful about how deeply I got into my sadness with the music at any given time. One day while I was listening to the chants I was in so much pain that I called my friend Shirley. She told me to just turn them off. I'd felt so lost in the pain at the time that I had not thought to do something so simple.

I suggest that you be aware of how deeply you can stay with the sadness at any given time. Sometimes it feels okay to go with the music and the feelings, and sometimes it does not and we get to turn it off. This is a metaphor for our whole process of grieving. When feelings of sadness are overwhelming, you can take an action—call a friend, make a meal, take a walk. Be in the sadness for a while and then remember you can take an action to turn it off when you need to. Of course, sometimes it is not that easy when a wave hits you, but know that sometimes an action can help.

Bob and I had loved the recording of "Time to Say Good-bye" by Andrea Bocelli and Sarah Brightman. We used to play it in the car and shed some tears. (Kaya and China had refused to ride with us if we played that tape any more). Maybe, on some level those moments were prophetic, but the music was important to us both. I played it some after Bob's death, and it helped me connect with him and with how sad it was that we had to say good-bye. (I haven't played it in years and feel no need to go back to that sadness in that way. I write this to let you know the sadness does subside.)

Chris had loved the Grateful Dead and had followed them all over the country. She was extremely sad when Jerry Garcia died in 1995. After she died, all Grateful Dead music made me cry. One of Chris's favorites was "Ripple." I listened to that song a lot when I was able. The part that always got to me was about a path that is for your steps alone, and if I knew the way, I would take you home. Joni Mitchell's songs also brought Chris back to me, and they still do sometimes.

Pause. Take Three Breaths. Consider: What was your loved one's favorite music? Can you allow yourself to listen to it yet? Can you determine when it's okay to play and when it might be too much for you? Do you have different favorite music that can be nurturing to you right now? If so, listen to it.

Finding Words from Them

As I went through papers after Bob died, I found cards or notes from him that made me cry; I felt the depth of my loss when I came across them. We had a ritual of making elaborate Valentines, more like collages, with phrases and pictures cut out from magazines or postcards. I came across a set of Valentines that we had made in the Caribbean one February. I put them in a scrapbook and would refer to it when I wanted to visit him and those feelings.

Over the course of my grieving, as I sorted through some of Chris's papers, I found a painful and amazing poem she had written to me when she was in her last treatment center. She had read it to me in therapy, and we had both cried and talked about it. When she was gone, it felt even more painful:

> *My pain pumps through my body*
> *Starting in my heart with a sob.*
> *To think of you not loving me*
> *As much as you loved a substance*
> *To think of the desertion of attention*
> *That I too didn't turn to human love for.*
> *It was a balance of total lies*
> *In my head I deny*
> *In my heart I cry*
> *For our tie was broken for long.*
> *We tried to be friends*
> *But my heart didn't mend.*
> *For the roles we never had*
> *The acting did the job.*
> *But it couldn't for long*
> *So I now*
> *Want us*
> *To be true.*
> *As we learn and we cry*
> *Our old selves will die*
> *And we can learn to be free.*

After her death, the poem felt prophetic and was even more heart wrenching.

Of course, the weight of the guilt about Chris's death was profound, but the deep sadness prevailed. How do you get out of bed when your daughter has written this to you, and within a year she overdoses? (In Chapter 8, we will address the specific problems of grieving a death from addiction or suicide.) The sadness of these kinds of losses is increased by the complications of deep guilt and blame and the mystery of who recovers and who does not.

Writing Out Your Sadness by Corresponding with Them

I would write to Bob and then Chris and then Bob again. I used a tool I had learned from my psychodrama training with my mentor, Tian Dayton: I could also write back from them and answer my own letters. This technique helped me a great deal, especially with Chris because our relationship was so incomplete and so sad.

Dear Chris,

I'm trying not to feel that you wasted your life, but it seems like you did waste a lot of it. I'm so glad you got to have Kaya and China. I'm angry that you left the way you did. I'm glad you didn't consciously kill yourself, but it was pretty close to that.

I miss you and I've missed you for years, even when you were alive. I remember when I went to be with you in the last rehab, how wonderful you were, sober and so honest and hopeful. I want to remember you that way.

Please follow the light. Let Bob help you now. I thought he could help you get sober, but this is how it happened. I can hardly believe it.

I need to know that you are OK. I'm sure you are. I will take care of Kaya and China and be committed to their care, but I need your help to get through this day.

Love, Mom

I found comfort and some peace in writing letters back from Chris.

Dear Mom,

I know I did waste a lot of time in my addiction. I'm so sorry I betrayed you, but you had also betrayed me. We were both sick, so maybe now we're even. I don't hold anything against you and I'm really OK. More than OK, even though I didn't mean to go.

But please take good care of Kaya and China for me. Give them a hug and a kiss and tell them I love them.

I love you, too, even though you were a tough mother to have. Now you have my girls to work things out with. Thank you for being my mother. Tell the girls I'm sorry.

Love, Chris.

Those made-up letters, in which I imagined how she would respond to my letters, were a godsend. I felt like I was channeling her, even though I was making it up as I went along. It's almost always a healing experience for anyone who tries it. I also used this tool with Bob, but with him I was so much more complete that it wasn't as necessary. I used it just when I missed him. When I suggest to friends or to clients that they write letters like this, I say, "You knew them really well. Consider that they are in their highest selves. How would they respond to your letter?"

WHEN SADNESS TURNS INTO DEPRESSION

I believe depression can be defined as getting stuck in some feelings when sadness takes over your life. This can and often does happen for a time. Sadness and depression are solitary experiences; no one can make the journey through them for you or even with you. Notice what you are thinking about yourself and the one you've lost, and see if you might have lost perspective. There were times when I felt like I didn't know which way was up, and I had to call a friend to set my thinking straight again. I would still feel sad, but not as lost in it.

You might also be stuck in some anger or guilt about your deceased loved one that has been unexpressed or unacknowledged. Be aware of what you are feeling. I needed to express my sadness and depression through a poem, a collage, or a letter. Some people need to just sit with it. Just be aware of what you are thinking or feeling if you get stuck.

One thing that can help you out of depression is action. Again, there is a fine balance between stillness, sitting with our painful feelings, and action. You might not want to get out of bed. Ask someone to take a walk with you if you feel too debilitated to go out alone. Walking outdoors can be so helpful for depression. I found walks on the beach comforting and nurturing at the same time. I would take Spunky to the beach, take a short walk along the shore, and drive home feeling so much better.

Of course, experiencing prolonged depression for more than a few weeks is when seeking out professional help is important. A counselor of any kind can be very helpful in dealing with depression, and a psychiatrist can evaluate your condition and prescribe antidepressant medication. I would suggest checking out both avenues if you are in a depression.

Pause. Take Three Breaths. Consider: How much have you been dealing with depressed feelings (inertia, lack of interest in life, lack of motivation, feelings of hopelessness)? Consider what you need when you feel like that: could you sleep, get some rest, take a walk outdoors, pick up a book, watch mindless TV, or call a friend (even though you won't want to)? How hard is it for you to reach out in times like this? How difficult is it for you to balance between inaction (sitting with yourself and your feelings) and taking actions? Pray for guidance if finding that balance is a big challenge for you. Would you consider getting some professional help?

GRIEF GROUPS

In my experience, it is difficult to find a helpful grief group. Hospice and the Cancer Society seem to have been most successful at establishing groups for the purpose of grieving. I have also found it difficult to form a grief group or workshop. People grieving are so vulnerable. To even think of joining a group about your loss can be very challenging. That is one of the reasons I decided to write this book: I want people to have a map of their journey and still have their solitude for a time. However, I do recommend ruthlessly pushing through any resistance and exploring the possibilities of joining a group for people in loss.

One of my hopes is that from reading this book, people will consider forming grief groups around the model of the 12-Step recovery program. See the Twelve Steps of Grieving at the end of this book, and see if you can get a few friends together to try it.

I personally used my regular 12-Step groups, which I had already been attending, as my grief group. Any ongoing support group you attend regularly can be used for your grieving, if you let it. A reading group or a meditation group can be used for support in your process, if you can share some of your feelings there and let yourself be known.

Professionally, I was in a training group with Tian Dayton that was focused on psychodrama. I did a lot of my deepest, saddest grief work in that group. I would pick someone to play the role of Bob or Chris and get to speak to them and process my feelings very directly. Then the person playing the deceased would share what it was like for him or her to play that role. It is a bold method, maybe ruthless, but it helped me enormously through my sadness. During the first year or two, I was able to travel through the pain and to emerge into knowing I would be able to go on without them.

MOVING ON

Out of the sadness and depression emerge the possibilities of acceptance and going on without them. At first, it's like a faint glimmer of light, then it gets a little brighter, and then you begin to have visions of the possibilities of a life without the person you've lost.

About a year after Paul died, my friend Susan was driving home one day when she began to think about what it felt like to arrive home and the comfort and joy of finding Paul there to greet her. She realized, as if for the first time, that Paul would never be there to greet her again. She pulled the car over and sobbed for a long time. That felt to her like the beginning of a deeper acceptance of his loss, and at that moment she had glimpses of what her new life could be without him.

What You Resist Persists

Let yourself dive into the feelings and swim around in them. Some people think we are more ourselves in the depth of this grieving process than we are in our usual lives. Immerse yourself in your feelings, and find other parts of you that you might not have known were there. A marker for your swim in the sadness is a sign that reads, "Look for the love," for you, for your loved one, or even for just being alive in that day.

You might find yourself in bed. You might find yourself with no energy. You might find yourself alone and bereft. You might find yourself unable to function. You might find yourself crying much more than before. But remember, you might also find yourself.

THINGS TO REMEMBER

- You will not always feel the way you do in the depths of your sadness.

- Don't let anyone stop your emotional life by accusing you of feeling sorry for yourself.

- Label your sadness as *feeling for yourself* or *having compassion for yourself.*

- As your grief progresses, you are likely to feel more deeply sad for some time. It gets harder before it gets easier.

- You won't want to do anything at times, so don't—and remember ruthlessness.

- Do not make any decisions in your sadness—not about yourself, your loved one who is gone, life, or God. Sadness will color your thinking for some time.

- Sadness needs expression. Go to your journal, make a mandala or a collage, write a poem, or write a letter to the person you've lost. The ruthless part of you can help you express your sadness even when you don't want to.

- Music can help in your sadness. Play music they liked or that you liked on your own. Use your judgment about how much you listen or when to turn it off. Play it when you feel safe enough to feel the sadness.

- Depression is getting stuck in your sadness. Be aware of what you are thinking and of what might feel unfinished that is making you feel stuck.

- Grief groups can be difficult to find. Consider looking for one to join or even finding a friend or two to form your own (using the Twelve Steps of Grieving).

- Know that grief is an expression of love and that there can be richness in the sadness of grief that can help you.

- Allow the depth of your sadness to move you toward acceptance.

CHAPTER 8

Grieving the Unheroic Death: Loss from Addiction or Suicide

Our full emotional spectrum is never more present than in our grief for an alcoholic, addict, or suicide. We try to make sense of a senseless death that almost always feels so unnecessary and preventable. Yet, it happened. We are not meant to take our own lives, but some people do. And the people around them are left to pick up the pieces.

Surviving a loss from suicide or addiction is a feat. Shock and denial can envelop the survivor for years. Many people get stuck in one phase or another. "We never changed anything in that room after he died" is a frightening place for anyone to live. When we don't know what to make of the shock and all the feelings, often we just let it sit there, untouched. We need to find the ruthless part of ourselves to face and survive this ruthless task.

Methods for grieving the death of an addict or suicide are the same as for any other process of grieving: journal writing, writing letters, writing back from your loved one, artistic activities, mandalas, collage, connecting with nature, looking at photos, and memorials. You need all the permissions as well: permission to be alive when your loved one is not, to be angry, to find ways to express anger safely, to obsess about the deceased, to feel guilty and work through that with someone else, to feel depressed and sad for a while, and to need and seek help.

When the addict or alcoholic dies, the need for all these methods is much more emergent and intense. The relationship is often extremely incomplete, and the trauma—often including lots of guilt and shame—is usually deep. Writing in a journal about your loss of the person you loved is an especially important method for keeping your process going, and it keeps you from losing yourself in this challenging journey, which can become very isolating. The shame and blame can feel torturous, and the feeling that no one fully understands can isolate you for a long time.

Pause. Take Three Breaths. Consider: Have you been close to anyone who died from addiction and/or suicide? How have the other people around them dealt with this kind of loss? Were they able to be open about the story? Do you suspect any losses around you to have been from these illnesses, but you were not told the truth? Have you felt a pull to bury the problem and not speak openly about what happened?

DENIAL

Losing someone you love to addiction or suicidal depression creates a most complex and ruthless grief. Witnessing the deterioration before your eyes of someone you love is like watching special effects in a horror movie, except this is real and in your own life. To be in the dark about what is really happening to your loved one and then to be suddenly faced with his or her demise is a horrifying shock.

In my experience, addiction and suicidal depression often occur together. When I hear of a suicide, I ask if the deceased was addicted to anything. While the answer is often yes, when it is no I frequently find out later that the survivor was in some denial about a heavy use of tranquilizers, pain pills, alcohol, or other drugs.

I opened the paper on May 17, 2012, to a headline about Robert Kennedy Jr.'s wife's death at home at age fifty-three. She was reported to have hanged herself in the family's barn. When I read on, I noticed that she'd had two DWIs the previous year: one for intoxication and the other for driving on pain medication.

Addiction and suicide often occur together. For me, the addiction explains the suicide, but depression can often "explain" the addiction, too. They almost always co-occur.

One can only imagine the deluge of painful feelings for family members that follows the suicide of an alcoholic mother of four who was about to get divorced. In the next day's paper I read that the families were fighting in court over the body and where she should be buried. I imagine it took those families a long, painful time to come to an acceptance of the realities of the fatal illness of depression and addiction that plagued that mother. I believe her suicide was no one's fault. I hope they got there.

As you deal with losing the alcoholic, addict, or depressive, you come to realize that many mistakes were made. However, when you deal with the shame (by telling the truth) and the blame and guilt (by doing the emotional work), all that is left is human frailty and the realities of having a fatal illness.

Eventually, as I write in Chapter 11, all that is left is the love, but that is at the conclusion of a harrowing emotional journey. Understanding and accepting the reality that your loved one was a flawed human with a fatal illness is an important start.

GUILT

Almost everyone who knew the addict feels guilty when he or she dies. Even people with more distant relationships, like neighbors, feel terrible about the deficits in their relationships: "I wish I had spoken to him more"; "I could see there was something wrong"; "I wish I hadn't been so distant, but I was turned off by her lifestyle"; "I wish I'd been more persistent or even just friendlier."

Of course, when you are close to someone who has been complicit in his or her own demise, the feelings avalanche. The death is usually sudden, even if addiction has been an issue for years and you knew he or she was in trouble. When Chris died, I had been afraid for years of receiving that call. When it came, there could be no preparation for the ruthless storm that news created in me.

Living with addiction is a slow suicide, but death is the rapacious creditor. How could death be a surprise when someone has been addicted to heroin for years? But it almost always is. Love is blind, and the heart knows no preparation, nor any reasoning, for the rude interruption of relationship.

I have heard it said that addiction betrays, and it does. When the initial shock subsides, it all feels like betrayal. Either I had betrayed my daughter, or she had betrayed me. And both were true on some levels.

Even if you have had to cut off contact, you have not betrayed your loved one. Cutting off contact often occurs because the addict or depressive is often impossible to be in relationship with. His or her behavior challenges the relationship at every turn, and the challenges only get worse as the addict or depressive deteriorates.

My granddaughter Kaya started to refuse her mother's calls when she was about nine years old. Since she was two, promises from her mother, like "I'll come visit you soon," were broken again and again, and Kaya began to feel her anger and was protecting herself from the deep hurt. When her mother died, I think she felt worse than if they'd been speaking regularly. I emphasized with her that her mother had been very ill, and that was why she died. Those words are cold comfort to a ten-year-old.

My son, Bill, had also stopped responding to his sister's desperate, drunken requests for money or other practical help. He had said to her, "I don't want to see you like this." Chris told me on the phone from California that she looked fine and didn't understand what he was talking about. She seemed genuinely confused about her brother's response. I referenced her drug use, but she was oblivious to her effect on anyone in her life. When she died suddenly, Bill's guilt was palpable. My son has had to work hard on himself for years to come through this ruthless journey to acceptance and enjoyment of his life today.

I had taken a middle ground with Chris. Whenever she called I would tell her I loved her and encourage her to get help in whatever city she was in. The calls I got from her when she lived in Hawaii were the worst. She would sound stoned and then put her three-year-old daughter on the phone. China would sing a line from the Joni Mitchell song "Carey." She only knew the part that repeats, "I like you, I like you, I like you." I felt so moved and yet impotent to do anything from so far away.

My denial was deep. Often, it is impossible to decipher the difference between denial and hope. I now see how much denial I was in. I had stopped giving Chris money, but I couldn't stop taking her occasional collect phone calls and being loving with her on the phone. Some addiction experts suggest cutting off all contact from the active person, but I could not bring myself to do that. Would she have woken up and gotten help if I had? I will never know. I actually cherish the little bits of contact I did have with her the year before she died, and I have mostly forgiven myself for any denial and enabling that was present in me.

After Chris died, I regretted almost everything I had done. "I should have been tougher. I should have refused her calls. I was such an enabler. I should have completely supported her. I should have gone to San Diego to rescue her. If I had given her money, she could have used it to get well." That last one was definitely more denial.

Talking to people who'd had similar losses was a godsend. My two biggest regrets went in opposing directions: "I should have been tougher" versus "I should have helped her more." I heard stories of people getting better with both approaches, and I heard about the deaths. Somehow, knowing there were mixed results from such differing approaches helped me in my grieving.

I still have bouts of self-doubt when I see the lingering effects of

Chris's death on her two young daughters. I see them struggling with their own sense of security and self-esteem, and I think, *I should have done more to save their mother. Or at least, I should have been a better mother myself.* A big part of my life today is giving my granddaughters the care I wish I could have given to their mother. I write more about that in the last section of this book, "Going on Without Them."

Pause. Take Three Breaths. Consider: Do you carry any guilt or shame about a suicide or addictive death in your life? What are some of the things you feel guilt about? Have you told people about this death and some of your feelings about it? Could you consider forgiving yourself for any mistakes you might have made? Would you write about it?

FINANCES

Money cannot save the addict or depressive from this severe illness and possible ultimate end. For a while, I paid half of Chris's rent to assuage my guilt and to feel that I could still help her. A mistake? I'm still not sure. After her death, I went through a period of deeply regretting that I didn't have more money. Someone I knew who had a suicidal, addicted teenager had flown her home from boarding school, paid for a great deal of therapeutic help for her, and sent her on a few exotic trips with a sober companion. Today, this young woman is healthy and sober, teaches history in a local high school, and just had her first baby. This all happened a few years after Chris's death, and I couldn't help the intense envy that came up in me when I heard this story.

On the other hand, another family with money gave their son every opportunity to get help by sending him to a long-term treatment center, and he died of an overdose a few months after he left the program. His family had given him as much help as any family could possibly give. In my grief, I heard many stories of wealthy families who had the same tragic end as my Chris. My father was right: "We all did the best we could."

Tough Realities

Tough love can work to help, but when the addict is locked out or rejected by his or her family, everyone is even more fraught with regret if the addict dies. I saw one family who could not recover from the death of their son and brother in the Philippines. He had gone there thinking he could stay off drugs because they were not accessible in that country. At Christmastime he called to ask his family to help him come home. They refused, thinking they should not enable him, thinking they were doing the right thing by making him face his problem and get the right kind of help where he was. But when they got notice from the Philippines that he'd overdosed and died a week later, they were inconsolable in their grief.

I was unable to intervene in this family's embittered sorrow. They were in severe conflict with each other and could not stop going back and forth with the blame and shame they were heaping on themselves and each other.

There are so many potentially "stuck" places on this harrowing path toward acceptance and resolution of grief. It is painful to witness a family or individual getting ensnared by one of them. I lost contact with this family, but do hope they found some solace and some peace.

Pause. Take Three Breaths. Consider: These are seemingly ruthless truths that must be taken in deeply as you travel through the forest of your sorrow:

- You cannot prevent a death from addiction or suicide.
- You do your best, and often that best is not enough to keep your loved one alive.

- Your loved one's death is not your fault.
- *You cannot keep anyone alive.*

Do you disagree with any of these statements? Would it be soothing or helpful to you if they were true? Take them in and consider accepting the truth of what I suggest to you.

TELLING THE TRUTH

Telling the truth about how the alcoholic, addict, or suicide died is most important to healing and recovering from this kind of loss. What we resist definitely persists, and managing the information about this kind of death could kill you. Dodging and going through the machinations of changing your story is exhausting. Holding a secret is corrosive; there is nothing to feel ashamed about.

What heals shame the most is telling the truth. The person you loved died of an illness as certainly as if he or she had developed cancer. Please work on having the courage to tell the true story of your loved one's end.

Pause. Take Three Breaths. Consider: How much shame or guilt do you feel about this death? What is that about? How honest have you been about what happened? Who have you spoken to most honestly? Could you give yourself permission to speak about it much more, if you need to?

Who Is Responsible?

We can't help looking for someone to blame for this tragedy. It is like playing "hot potato" with the searing pain. Whose fault is this? "It must be mine. No, it must be yours." The list can be very long: their doctors, their therapists, their rehab, their parents, their siblings, their children, their friends, God, anyone who ever hurt them, or yourself. I went back and forth, pinning Chris's death on her rehab and her father and then back on myself for many months.

We had all made mistakes, but the rage was intense and had no mercy. "It was me—it was her" can feel endless, and sometimes it is if we don't reach out for help.

The anger often lingers. I went through days of rage at Chris, although I simultaneously would see her as a victim (which didn't help anyone before or after her death). When my anger at her hit, it was a shock to my system. I felt that I had no right to be so angry with my dead daughter. Yet I had gone through hell with her for years; for example, when she would go missing for months and having to deal with all the disruptions in her daughters' lives. After I had put her out, she broke into my house so often that I had to hire a surveillance service to protect my home from my own daughter and her friends.

And when she died, my angry thoughts were all over the map: *She could have tried harder; she could have worked harder at AA; she should have stayed in the East where people knew and loved her; she was so willful and outrageous; she should have expressed her anger more directly instead of taking it out on herself (and the whole family); she did this to herself; she did this to me.*

Pause. Take Three Breaths. Consider: Where does your anger want to go about this loss? To him or her? To you? To someone else? Would you consider writing some letters you won't send, or just writing about it? How have you dealt with your anger? Are there any wounded or broken relationships with people who are still alive, that need some healing or repair? Would you work on those more? How have some of these unresolved feelings affected you?

DEPRESSION

I remember meeting the houseguest of a friend several years after she had lost her son to an overdose. She seemed quite distant and shut down emotionally; I told her our mutual friend had shared with me that we had something deep in common in our histories, and I thought maybe we could talk about it. She said, "I don't need to, but if you do, I will." Sensing the wall I had just encountered, I responded, "No, that's okay." I felt sad for her, and I imagined she was frozen somewhere in the tundra of her unresolved grief. Maybe she was just taking care of herself in the moment, but I sensed she was closed off from connection and the rest of her emotional life.

Unaddressed feelings and unresolved grief persist if they are continually pushed down. Just this year, my friend Fran told me she felt like she had been living under a cloud of her brother's suicide for over thirty years. She could not get through the anger she felt because her brother had jumped in front of a subway in New York City just two days after she had given birth to her second son. The pall that his death had put over her family felt to her like something impossible to recover from. Fran said the anger she felt about what he'd done had colored much of her experience with her newborn son and then continued like a festering wound for thirty years.

Her brother had been an alcoholic who refused treatment. He had been engaged to be married, but in hindsight appeared to be a closeted gay man. Fran's own drinking increased dramatically after he died. She told me she was unable to forgive him, or to acknowledge how ill he had been, until she got treatment herself for her own addictions. Over time, with help and being in her own recovery process, she gained empathy and even forgiveness for the brother she had loved.

A few months after Chris died, I had a huge argument with my friend Shirley. She said, "You are still blaming Chris for her illness." I was furious, and I raged at her through my tears. "You don't understand what it's like to lose someone you love to addiction. It feels like she could have tried harder to get well and that she was self-destructive and irresponsible." Shirley held firmly to her position, and over time I have seen that she was right. I have had to

145

come further in forgiving my daughter for being so ill and have had to forgive myself for the parts that I played in her illness.

Shirley may not have understood all aspects of my grief in that moment, but the gift she gave me about not blaming my daughter was priceless. Anger wants to blame, but it can be excruciating to blame your loved one for an untimely death after he or she is gone.

I had the personal experience of a suicide a few years after Chris's death. My friend Jane had a son who was addicted to heroin. She and I had been in a support group together when our kids were teenagers, and we'd connected over the challenges of having addicted offspring. She and her husband had been in and out of treatment with their son since he was a young teenager. I got a call from a mutual friend one winter night that Jane's son had overdosed and that she and her husband were flying to Atlanta the next day to arrange the funeral.

I called her but got her answering machine. I left a message that I wanted to help her through this, and that I knew she could survive it. She didn't return my call, but I knew she was out of town for the funeral.

A week later, I got a call that she had killed herself in her apartment.

It was an icy shock. Jane was a therapist who had done a lot of work on herself and also on her family. She had worked in the healing professions all her life, and so had her husband. They had both helped many people, and they seemed to be a very spiritual, conscious couple. I hadn't pursued her as much as I might have, thinking I would connect with her after they got back from Atlanta. Of course, I felt guilty.

Jane was not an alcoholic nor addicted to anything that I knew about. I think she was an exception to my theory of the co-occurrence of addiction and suicide. She was probably medicated in her grief, but that was not unusual. The night she and her husband came home from the funeral, apparently she set up an altar honoring her son, wrote a long suicide note to her daughter, took all the pills in the house, and died lying in front of her son's altar.

Jane had temporarily lost her mind with grief. She simply lost all perspective. I later found out her marriage had been in trouble for quite some time. I had not known about that or I probably would have been more active in pursuing her. She was a very private person, and I thought she had her husband close by.

At Jane's funeral, I was one of the many friends who spoke. I said I understood what Jane had done. I don't support suicide, but I could see how momentarily she could not imagine living with the knowledge of her son's tragic death. Another person spoke about how Jane had taught him to survive his feelings and that feelings change as you allow them to move through you. He expressed anger that she had not given herself a chance to survive her own.

TAKE NOTHING PERSONALLY

The Four Agreements, a book by Don Miguel Ruiz, lists four spiritual axioms; one of them is TAKE NOTHING PERSONALLY. The arc of my daughter's life was not about me. I needed to get my anger out, but ultimately her death was her own. Al-Anon teaches "Live and Let Live." I came to the idea of "Live and Let Die," which is a ruthless attitude, but one that I believe saved my life.

The feelings of anger, guilt, and remorse last a long time. I once heard a spiritual teacher say that we die when we are supposed to die. When a friend of mine lost her son in his twenties, she went to Egypt where she heard about the Book of the Dead, an ancient Egyptian funerary text that consists of prayers intended to assist a dead person's journey through the Duat, or underworld, and into the afterlife. Those ancients believed that the day of your death is written in the book on the day of your birth. My friend found a great deal of solace in that idea, and she passed it on to me when I needed it. I came to believe that both Bob and Chris died when they were meant to die and that their deaths basically had nothing to do with me.

There are no accidents. I wanted to believe that, but I couldn't for a long time. On a bad day, I still don't. Here is a poem I wrote when an old pang of guilt came over me last summer:

> The sprinkler spurts around the lawn.
> I move it—no buried system for me.
> The grass gets brown where it doesn't reach.
> What parts of me, browned in neglect.
>
> You killed your daughter—
> No, not true.
> But you were not responsible
> To the role of mother,
> To the children entrusted to your care.
>
> Chris is dead,
> And I was not responsible.
>
> The water whooshes on the parched grass.
> I pull the hose to the next browning patch.
> Today I am responsible.
> And I was not responsible.
> And I was responsible.
> And the grass is still not greening.
>
> Whoosh.
> I cry and let the sprinkler do its job.
> Watering my brown patches in the sun.

The pain never completely goes away. It subsides and is usually not in the forefront. The scars are there, and then I do the next right thing, and I can live with myself . . . most of the time.

A RUTHLESS JOURNEY

There was no amount of knowledge that could have prepared me for the searing pain of losing my daughter. Having someone you love die from addiction, without dignity, with the sickening feeling that she had been complicit in her own demise, makes the grief much more complicated. I felt at times I couldn't go on, and I wanted to die with her rather than feel the shame and profound disappointment.

After Chris died, I entered an emotional landscape that felt more dangerous than anything I had ever experienced, even growing up in my alcoholic family. It felt like a field of landmines interspersed with pockets of quicksand. Explosions of rage and blame seemed to come out of nowhere, followed by boggy, sinking feelings of drowning in depression and self-hatred. There seemed to be no rhyme or reason to the sequences, and I felt totally at the mercy of my internal roller coaster.

I had lived my life on a daily basis for many years, but now I had to take it moment to moment. I had to give myself permission to be alive. At first, I was not able to be alone very much. I definitely needed my friends around me constantly, and I reached out a lot. Fortunately, I have close friends who also knew to check in on me frequently.

There is a kind of healthy ruthlessness that comes in the course of a deep grieving, cutting through many things as unimportant and everything as cancelable. Talking with friends helped me sort out what was important and what was distorted by my turbulent emotions.

The pitfalls of isolation and self-hatred were numerous. I was embarrassed to cry. Mostly I needed people, so I wouldn't think too much or rehash the past alone in my mind. On my own I was often self-hating or morbid, thinking of Chris's body and what she had done to it or what condition it was in now, or blaming her or someone else. I made a huge case against myself as a bad mother and was convicted and sentenced on a daily basis.

The shame about Chris's death was almost paralyzing, making it very tough to get out of bed, especially right after the funeral. Although I had worked with alcoholism and drug addiction as a disease for decades, gotten sober myself sixteen years earlier, been involved with 12-Step programs, and had learned a lot about the nature of this fatal illness, when it came to losing my daughter, guilt and self-recrimination poured into me. It was as if I forgot that it was a disease that killed her. I felt like I should have been able to prevent this tragedy and that I had failed miserably as both a mother and as a professional healer.

GIVING MEANING TO LOSS

A few months after Chris died, the Twin Towers came down in New York City. My thought was that my towers, Bob and Chris, had come down several months before. I decided to write about unheroic deaths from addiction and suicide, and how people get through them. I wanted Chris's death, and what I had experienced with both losses, to help other people. I felt that as soon as I heard she was dead. I said it when I gave the eulogy at her funeral, and it gave me some solace in dealing with what felt like such a senseless and unnecessary loss.

My son, Bill, is a writer, and he offered to help me with the book. Within that first year we started interviewing people who were grieving the loss of addicts. I gave those interviews a lot of energy, even traveling to California to meet with the widow of actor Carroll O'Connor (of Archie Bunker fame), who had lost her actor son to an overdose and then her husband, Carroll, to a heart attack five years later.

Although we abandoned the project before publication, I found a lot of help for myself and for my relationship with my son in the interviewing process and in processing what we'd heard. I spoke with mothers whose hearts were broken like mine, daughters whose mothers had drunk themselves to death, and a woman whose brother, a state Supreme Court judge in a western state, had overdosed on heroin in a hotel room in Las Vegas.

Bill got an interview with former presidential candidate George McGovern, who had previously written *Terry: My Daughter's Life-and-Death Struggle with Alcoholism*. The candor in his description of his understanding of how his daughter died was very helpful to me. She had frozen to death in a parking lot after passing out from drinking.

McGovern's honesty about the circumstances of his daughter's death helped ease my shame about the way my daughter had died. Here was a well-known politician, a man who had run for president, whose daughter left the world the same way Chris did. Mr. McGovern admitted in the book that he felt terrible remorse about neglecting his family. He even regretted his political career and running for president because it had kept him from being an involved father, especially with Terry, with whom he'd been close.

This didn't, of course, entirely erase my shame or guilt. I continued to wish that I had gotten Chris's phone call from jail the weekend before she overdosed as well as many other things. However, the way George McGovern had come to terms with the loss of his daughter, and the honest responsibility he took for the mistakes he had made with her, helped me stop linking Chris's death with my flawed mothering. His book also helped me not to feel ashamed of the way my daughter had died.

When the Twin Towers came down, I felt as if the whole country had caught up with how I had been feeling for months. Now everyone was grieving and bereft. However, there was a palpable difference between the outpouring of grief for the innocent victims of 9/11—many of whom spent their last day in heroic acts of bravery—and the tangle of conflicting feelings that was my grief. My thirty-two-year-old daughter, Chris, was not sitting at her desk at work when a plane flew into the building, nor had she kissed her two daughters good-bye as they left for school that morning, nor had she died heroically in the line of duty of any kind. She died of a heroin and alcohol overdose. She died with a needle in her arm under a freeway in San Diego. The initial wave of despair that washed over me seemed like more than I could bear, just as I'm sure many of the survivors of 9/11 felt. However, it was all compounded by the circumstances of her death, by guilt and shame and regret.

HEALING FROM THE UNHEROIC DEATH

I used several specific healing methods to get through the loss of my addicted daughter. They were psychodrama (a specific, very creative psychotherapy method), Al-Anon (a self-help support group designed for the support of families of alcoholics and addicts), the practice of gratitude, and the practice of accepting and living with regrets.

Psychodrama

I had been part of a psychodrama group for many years. It's part therapy supervision and part psychotherapy for the participants. After Bob died, I was able to do dialogues with him by doing work in group therapy sessions about it. I would pick someone to play Bob and tell him how much I missed him or express anything I hadn't been able to tell him while he was alive. He and I were quite complete, but I did at least two dramas about Bob's death, and they advanced my healing from the pain of losing him.

The situation was different with Chris. I had worked in group therapy for years about her addiction and her abandonment of her two daughters. I remember one piece of work years before she died in which I declared to the person playing her that I had obsessed about her funeral long enough, that the funeral was cancelled: "No more thoughts of funerals," I told her.

After the real funeral, I was bereft, and I took all my feelings to this psychodrama group. I remember one therapy scene in which someone playing "Ed" and I were arguing with each other, and Chris's dead body was between us, lying on the floor. I raged at "Ed" and made him walk away, and then I embraced "Chris" and got to say good-bye to her—a proper, lengthy good-bye. Of course, there wasn't a dry eye in the room.

People's caring and feedback about what they were feeling helped knit me back together. I remember someone saying she would have loved to have a mother like the mother I became after I got sober. Her mother had died drunk, so her identification and empathy with my work was on many levels at once. I also remember that there were two women in the group who had not gotten to have a child. They envied me having Chris in my life, even though she had died tragically at thirty-two. Those moments stayed with me and became part of the fabric of my emotional life for years to come.

Al-Anon

I went to Al-Anon for several years in the course of my own emotional recovery from my alcoholic family. Al-Anon is a 12-Step program, based on the principles of Alcoholics Anonymous, for the relatives and friends of alcoholics and addicts. The basic message of Al-Anon is to keep the focus on yourself. You can't control an addict, but you can surrender to your own powerlessness and control your emotional reactions to the addict's choices and behavior. Living with addiction in the family is extremely destabilizing and pulls one away from one's own center. There is ruthlessness to the Al-Anon approach. Some people call it "Black Belt Al-Anon" because even when someone around you is in turmoil, the only real solution is ruthless self-care.

I discovered that keeping the focus on myself and on being alive was essential to my bereavement process. It was easy to get stuck in what other people thought and even in what other people were experiencing in their grief. Although, of course, I did my best to help, I even had to distance myself at times from the grief experienced by my granddaughters, Kaya, who was ten, and China, who was six, and my son, Bill. I had to help myself before I could help them.

The Al-Anon slogan, "Live and Let Live," had helped me for years. When I realized the emphasis needed to be on the "live" part, it allowed me to let other people live their lives the way they had chosen. As I mentioned earlier in this chapter, I discovered in my grieving process that this slogan still applied, but it was now "Live and Let Die." When I first thought of it, I even heard the loud, thumping music of the original theme song for the old James Bond movie. It may sound cruel and heartless, but it was some of the best wisdom I found about how to get through my losses.

Gratitude

The concept of becoming grateful for having someone in your life for the time you did is very healing and powerful. At first, it was extremely hard for me to reach because of all the pain associated with Chris's life and with her death. But gradually, over time, I was able to develop gratitude for being Chris's mother and the enriching and challenging life experiences she gave me.

I keep in mind that Chris was basically a lovely young woman. She loved her friends, adored babies and animals, worked for Greenpeace, and taught me about being conscious of the environment and many other New Age consciousness experiences, like African dancing and drumming circles. She enjoyed creating things: she made her own jewelry, quilted, and was always working on some creative project. She had a big heart and was extremely sensitive and intuitive—a good person. I was able to remember those realities of who Chris really was, beyond her illness of addiction.

Over time I have been able to practice some gratitude for getting to be her mother and for being a part of her very difficult life.

Accepting and Living with Regrets

I couldn't type fast enough to express all the regrets I had after Chris's overdose. I deeply regretted all the things I hadn't done to help her, and paradoxically (and at the same time) all the help I had given her. I do have to say that I regretted not helping more than the help I had given. The ambivalence is best exemplified by the heavy conflicts Bob and I were faced with in dealing with our beloved granddaughters.

When Kaya was born, Bob and I were very involved in helping with her care. Chris was a loving mother who nursed her baby in a beautiful, natural way, took her everywhere, and seemed fulfilled in her motherhood role. However, within the first year of Kaya's life, Chris started drinking and drugging again, and her marriage broke up abruptly.

She left Kaya with us for long periods of time, and I finally went to court to take custody from her, really to protect Kaya from her mother's out-of-control behavior. One morning Chris had arrived at my house very drunk, with the baby in her arms. I felt I had to take action, and I did. I was sure that losing Kaya would wake Chris up from her addictive fog and that she would want help, but she did not.

This is the kind of bind that families experience with active addiction. Being caring and helpful in almost any way feels like cosigning their destructive behavior, while not helping feels like rejection and neglect. The prevailing wisdom is mostly not to help, but when a child is involved that can be a harrowing resolve.

Mike, Kaya's father, was eventually ready to take full custody of his daughter when she was about three, and we went back to court. During this time, Chris had a new boyfriend and gave birth to China. Bob and I decided to be more hands-off with China, even though we were already attached to her and loved her. We decided that we had been too helpful and possibly enabling with Kaya and taken over too much responsibility from Chris, thus enabling her to continue in her addiction. We thought that maybe having more responsibility for China would allow Chris to become more healthy and appropriate and not rely on us for substitute parenting so much. We were also a little worn out with childcare responsibilities and afraid for our own futures.

When China was six months old, Chris broke up with the baby's father and moved to Hawaii. Apparently, she set up a good life for herself for a short while, but within a year she had picked up again. She would visit for the holidays or during the summer, and she seemed okay until her last visit, when China was three. She was obviously using, and we had some very drunken scenes during that Christmastime. I deeply regret not intervening, at least to take China away from her. But we decided not to interfere.

By the following December, Chris was willing to go to rehab, and China came to live with us. By then China had experienced much abuse and neglect, and the whole family rallied around her. Chris went off to treatment in Florida, but left after a year and immediately was active in her addiction again. That time, we protected China and kept her up north with us.

One of my deepest regrets was returning China to her mother when Chris had almost a year of sobriety. By then she was in sober living and could accommodate her daughter. The treatment center and my ex-husband were against it, but Bob and I were feeling desperate to get our lives back, and Chris seemed to be doing quite well. In hindsight, I think Bob was already getting sick with cancer. Chris was also begging to get China back, and I felt it would be good for them both. It was impulsive and willful on my part, and Chris had picked up within a week of having China in her care.

We do make serious mistakes in dealing with the alcoholic or addict. The conflicting feelings are often severe, and sometimes we give in to what the addict wants or to our own needs that might not be productive in the long run. After Chris died, I can't tell you how many times I felt pain about having put China and Chris on that plane back to Florida and what a terrible mistake I had made. Of course, she could have picked up anyway, but she had had a lot of motivation to get well when she was working hard to get her daughter back. All that seemed to vanish once she had China with her.

The prevailing wisdom is to detach and walk away if the addict refuses help. That is mostly what we did in the last year of Chris's life, when we knew Kaya and China were both safe (Kaya with her father and China with Bob and me). This is where it completely makes sense that addiction is an illness. Chris's values deteriorated so quickly whenever she was using drugs and alcohol. It was like she became a different person. But the wreckage she created was very painful to witness and impossible to stop.

Of course, my role modeling as a mother had been atrocious. But I know families that were far more stable than ours, parents in intact marriages, no substance abuse in the family, with very similar stories where one offspring goes off the rails and descends into addiction. Those stories helped me after Chris died, and I came to see the disease aspect of what happens.

Parts of this illness remain a mystery to me. And the "luck" factor that George McGovern wrote about seems very real. The death of actor Philip Seymour Hoffman is a powerful example of the mystery of what kills the addict and how difficult it is to understand. When someone looks like they have everything to live for and their addiction kills them anyway, it is impossible to understand.

The families of addicts and alcoholics walk a fine line to remain loving and kind to the addict while not cosigning their behavior. Someone said to me recently that we have to work against our natural tendency to be helpful and caring in order to take care of ourselves and to give the alcoholic the best chance of recovery.

I cannot say that I am over my daughter's death, but I have come through a passage that was an amazing journey. I have written my heart out, cried my eyes out, been angry with God, and asked for help from many friends, professionals, and from God. I have also told the truth to everyone I could. My daughter did not die in a heroic way, or even in a way that most people would respect, but I have come to some peace about the way she died and about the way she lived.

The wreckage that is left after an unheroic death is extreme. It isn't natural to fight over bodies or to stop talking to one another after a loss. The film *In the Bedroom*, about the loving couple who split up after their son died in his addiction, was cold comfort. Spiritually, I came to accept that addiction is an illness and that it kills people. This illness killed my daughter, and I am grateful that it didn't kill me. There is cold comfort in ruthless grieving, but in the end, that's part of what is left when someone you love dies an unheroic death.

THINGS TO REMEMBER

- When the addict, alcoholic, or suicide dies, almost everyone around him or her feels guilty.

- That guilt can lead to blame and shame and managing information about how he or she died.

- Tell the truth about how your loved one died or you will be feeding the shame.

- A death from suicide or addiction involves a more complex set of feelings and is more difficult on many levels. It is always sudden and incomplete. It requires more intense emotional work and often therapeutic action.

- Remember that your loved one died of an illness as real as cancer or any physical disease. We don't blame a person, or his or her loved ones, if someone dies of cancer. Treat this death with the same respect.

- The addict's death is not your fault or the fault of anyone else. It is not even the fault of the person who died, but anger at your loved one is part of the process of grieving the addict or suicide.

- Talking to someone else who has experienced this kind of loss can be helpful and mutually healing.

- Reach out for professional help when just talking to others is not helping enough. Or try going to Al-Anon.

- There is no definite way to treat the addict or alcoholic that is foolproof. Tough love is suggested but is almost impossible to do perfectly. Even people who were not enabled can die.

- The addict or alcoholic can die in diverse circumstances, and you will be unable to figure out why it happened, although you will try.

- The death of a loved one to suicide or addiction *is not your fault. Take nothing personally.* People may try to blame you. *Do not take it on.* Again, *it is not your fault.*

CHAPTER 9

Identity, Roles, and Grief: Beyond Cultural Expectations

There has been a lot written and talked about regarding the work of forming our identity as we develop from children into adults. One of the major ways we establish and experience our own identity is through the people we are connected to in our lives, through the roles they play with us and we with them. I was a wife and a mother. But what happened to that identity when my husband died or when I was no longer a mother of a daughter alive on the planet?

As we discussed in Chapter 4, "I'd be lost without them" turns out to be quite literal when we experience a close loss. "Who am I without my mother (or my daughter, or my spouse) in my life?" can become a difficult question to answer and one that requires some deep thought and emotional awareness.

In psychology, role theory is a way of describing human behavior according to how we fill and fulfill a role. It provides a way of examining a relationship in a less personal way and gives a different perspective of the culturally defined and expected behaviors in any relationship. It helps us examine how the role affected the deeper emotional interactions and our sense of self. How creative we are in our roles is often connected to how satisfying those roles are for us and how they have enhanced us.

During the grieving process, when the obsessive "what-ifs" subside and the regrets begin to fade, when we've pinned blame on everyone and everything we can think of, and when we've shed the tears we have and given ourselves permission to experience all of our feelings and to go on without them, we will use this psychological concept of roles to take another look at where—and more important, who—we are without them.

I was recently speaking to a man who had lost his college-age son who said he did not want to be identified as the man who was grieving his son. Unfortunately, that is what happens for a time. We don't want to use our reluctance to being perceived that way as a reason not to grieve or to face the pain and discomfort of being that person. Actually, being identified as someone in deep loss is how we will be perceived and how we might experience ourselves, for as long as it takes to get through the grieving process.

I can tell you that today I do not identify as someone grieving, because I am not. I am no longer that person mourning my loved ones. Yes, I am someone who has experienced deep loss, but that is not how I experience myself today. A griever is not who you will be after you have gone through the grieving process. You will emerge from the other side of loss changed in some essential ways, more whole and more yourself, but not a perennial griever. Yes, some aspects of your identity will change, hopefully in the direction of more freedom to be fully yourself, and possibly less defined by the roles you play.

To make this journey, you need to take another, deeper look at your relationship with the one who died and a deeper look at your relationship with yourself and the world. You need to sort out who you are and want to be now that the role you played with the person who died no longer exists.

EXAMINING OUR ROLES

Examining the roles we played with our loved ones is a way to first examine our own identity when our loved ones were alive and then explore what is left of us after they leave the planet. We notice and appreciate the positive ways we related to our loved ones, and we often begin to appreciate how well we did with each other. We look at the roles we played with our loved ones and how poorly or creatively we fulfilled ourselves in those roles.

In grief, we need to shift some aspects of our identity. We ask ourselves, "Who was I with my loved one, and who am I now without him or her?" We are also led to consider who we might be or would wish to be without them.

Pause. Take Three Breaths. Consider: What role did you play with your lost loved one? How do you feel about that role? How well suited were you to play that role? How well suited was your loved one in the role he or she played with you?

Looking at the Dark Side

Psychotherapists have been called "Love's Executioner" because we find it necessary to give voice to the darker aspects of relationships. A noted psychologist, Irvin D. Yalom, wrote a book with that title. He describes the therapist's task of revealing the distortions and fantasies about love to the therapy client. The distorted aspects of any relationship are the feelings that are the most difficult to accept when someone dies. Psychotherapists help clients examine those distortions (execute the fantasy of "the love") to help people achieve emotional balance and a realistic sense of themselves and their relationships.

Playing a role can cause us to restrict our behavior. Unspoken expectations often come with a role, and sometimes that can feel oppressive. For example, I was a very emotional and loving mother, but one who was extremely unprepared for the responsibilities of parenthood. I was distracted by my very late adolescence (in my thirties) and by the changes in the culture that were exploding all around me. I mistakenly rejected (or at least was ambivalent about) the traditional role of mother, as I rejected the role of Westchester housewife. My children were caught in the crossfire, especially my female child. I often think of the wonderfully descriptive song from *Fiddler on the Roof* called "Tradition." It musically expresses some of the more oppressive aspects of traditional roles.

Resentments you might have experienced in the relationship can be connected to the limitations of the role you played and not about the other person at all. The term *merry widow* comes to mind. That term is about the new freedom widows can experience when regaining some freedom from the limitations of the traditional marital role they played. The term says very little or nothing about the actual quality of the marriage itself but alludes to the oppression that can be involved in playing any role.

At the same time, you can come to a place of realizing what a great job you did as a wife or mother and how much you love that role. Sometimes, this appreciation is not the first you have after a loss, but it can be a large aspect of what you are missing. By now you know that I suggest giving yourself permission to experience some "unacceptable" feelings after the loss of your loved one, which is part of ruthless grief.

I use the term *flawed human* a lot. Grief puts you up against your human flaws and the flaws of the person who has died. Through your grieving, you can reach a place where you begin to accept both your flaws and those of the other person, and you come to see that overall, and in most instances, you did a fairly good and a humanly flawed job. It is an important part of coming to acceptance.

Pause. Take Three Breaths. Consider: How comfortable were you with the role you played with your loved one? How creatively did you fill that role? What do you miss about having that role in your life? What challenges or regrets do you have about the role you played or the role your loved one played with you?

Loss of a Partner

When you are a spouse or committed partner, you self-identify through the lens of that all-encompassing role. It often defines the deepest aspects of how you see yourself. Losing that aspect of your identity can be extremely destabilizing; the term *widow* or *widower* is pervasive.

Until Bob died when I was fifty-eight, I had never been single for any length of time. I had married my childhood sweetheart, and a major part of my identity from the time I was sixteen years old was as someone's girlfriend or wife. I remember feeling a little desperate when Ed and I would break up for a time while we were dating, and then again after the divorce. I almost felt like I didn't have a valid existence unless I had a man at my side.

I am grateful that much of that attitude has changed in our culture, that men and women can have a valid life in this society without being in a committed partnership with another person. However, those beliefs and biases still exist on some levels, and they were triggered and then resurfaced in me when Bob died.

Suddenly I found myself asking, "Who am I without him? Who am I without a man in my life who is committed to me and I to him?" I could only clearly look at those questions after I had gone through my emotional work for a time.

Our marriage had been quite creative, meaning of our own creation. After Bob died, I had to look at and write about the feelings I had about my role as Bob's wife and about my new role as a single person. I was not someone's wife or even girlfriend. I was now a widow.

Bob and I did not enact all the typical husband-and-wife behaviors. We were both fairly independent, although we also relied on each other a fair amount. We spent at least one day a week apart: I'd go out to the country a day ahead of him to see a few clients there and to spend some time with Kaya, my precious little granddaughter. He would arrive on Friday, after he finished work in the city. One time he met a woman on the bus who commented on how nice it was that I went out a day ahead to get the house ready for his arrival, "to fluff the pillows," she said. It was a running joke with us that I was not a pillow fluffer and that we each had to fluff our own.

After Bob died, I had a strange combination of guilt and pride about how I had been as a wife. In my first marriage, I had cooked three meals a day for fourteen years, even though I always worked outside the home and was not an especially good cook. With Bob, I had been determined not to become resentful, nor to play the same rigidly defined role again, and I mostly did not.

Bob loved to tell the story of our first date at my apartment in New York. I invited him over for dinner, and when he arrived, I proudly showed him my collection of takeout menus and asked what he would like to have for dinner. He looked a little shocked, but we ended up having a lovely Thai meal from one of my favorite restaurants, and the evening was fun. Over the years, he joked that he should have known then that he was in trouble.

After he died, I had the odd feeling of not really knowing my "position in society" as a single woman. I had to get more comfortable in myself to be in the world as myself. Through my training as a therapist and from my own work, I was very aware of codependency, of the tendency to overdefine ourselves by who we love or are closest to. Now I had to face that distorted dependency within myself.

There is a saying that you know more about the codependent's partner than about the person you are with. When someone asked me, "How are you doing?" my answer might be "Bob is studying for his MSW." That is not uncommon. After Bob's passing, I had no one to tell about but myself (although I did continue this behavior by talking about my children and grandchildren, maybe more than usual). We come to rely on these roles in our lives, and when they are eliminated by a loss, we often flail around some as we search for meaning or definition of who we are without that position in society.

Pause. Take Three Breaths. Consider: How comfortable are you without the roles you and your deceased loved one played with each other? Do you resent anything about how your loved one was in his or her role with you?

Loss of a Parent

Before I lost my parents, I had already done most of my processing about those relationships in the course of my own therapy and recovery work. Some of the challenges you experience after parents pass are related to how much or how little you have examined your relationship with them before they died. Some of us have looked long and hard at the plusses and minuses of those relationships, and some have not. (You can substitute "parental figure" for "parent" if you were not raised by your biological parents.) Often your challenges will relate to how much you had established your identity apart from your parent before he or she died. If your parent lived to an older age, you are then thrust into the role of being an elder in the family.

Many things happen that can cause conflict and alienate a parent/offspring connection. Many people do not do a great job with the role of parent; I, myself, did not. This puts a lifetime burden on the offspring to come to terms with the assets and liabilities of how their parents performed in that role. There is often a tendency to feel guilty about how you treated your parents, especially if you view the relationships through the lens of traditional roles and of the perfection portrayed by the media (think *Ozzie and Harriet* or *Father Knows Best*). No one has the "ideal" relationship, and there are almost always some resentments, guilt, or regrets.

In general, the healthier and more whole the relationship was, the easier it is to let a parent go. In many ways, it is similar to dealing with the aftermath of a child who leaves home for school: the ones who have the most conflict or problems at home are the ones who have the most difficulty with separation anxiety when they leave the nest.

Some parent/child relationships are overly dependent and enmeshed. Of course, the age we are when a parent dies is most relevant to how dependent we were on them. When we are ten years old, we are not overly dependent on a parent, but just appropriately so.

Helicopter mom is a popular term right now. It describes parents who are overly enmeshed in their children's lives and hover too close. That kind of relationship has its own problems in grief. Giving yourself permission to be alive when your parent is not can be very challenging to those who were overly close to a parent.

Pause. Take Three Breaths. Consider: How would you describe yourself in the role of son or daughter? How comfortable was that role for you? What were the challenges? How comfortable do you think your mother or father was in the role of parent? How did that affect you? Remember to look for compassion for yourself, in or out of that role, and then compassion for your parent. Do you have regrets? Do some writing about the roles and what you miss.

We have all filled the role of offspring in some manner in our lives. How we filled that role has a lot to do with how our parents approached their roles with us. Many parents are ill equipped to raise a child due to their own limitations (such as youth, financial difficulties, substance abuse). A parent's deficits affect how his or her offspring develop and how those children experience their roles as sons or daughters. In grief, we are left to deal with any unresolved aspects of our experience with each of them and how it has affected the way we see ourselves today.

Your Relationship with Your Parents

There are many external definitions of *son* or *daughter,* but look deep inside and see how you really feel about how you were with your parents and what you might miss now that one or both of them is gone.

Sometimes when a parent has died, adult children feel more internal freedom to become authentically themselves and to free themselves of any constrictions that were involved in playing the role of son or daughter to that parent. In contrast, some offspring can feel a decrease of external controls, letting out some destructive impulses that their parent's presence in their lives helped keep at bay. In those cases, the griever may cause some havoc in his or her own life and the lives of family members, even going into some adolescent rebellion for a time.

My Parents and My Family System

I was the first grandchild and an only child for fourteen years before my brother was born. I was uncomfortable in my role as a daughter; one reason was because of alcoholism in the family and the destabilizing feelings that it triggered. (I learned later that both my mother's mother and my father's father were alcoholic.) My identity was deeply enmeshed with theirs. What was modeled for me as a child in the 1950s colored my perceptions of my mother and my parents' relationship. My mother was a servant to my dad, and she resented it and loved it at the same time. I resented my father for treating my mother with disrespect, and I hated that she let herself be treated in that way. There was a part of my mother that reminded me of Edith Bunker with Archie in *All in the Family*. I deeply resented her for that female servant mentality.

As my parents aged, I matured and gained some perspective on them and my relationship with them. Today, I am grateful I had time to develop and mature enough to see them from an adult perspective. I remember a very important moment that helped me see them in a different way. One day when I was complaining to a friend about something concerning my relationship with my parents, my friend said, "Your parents are people of their generation. They aren't particularly distant or controlling." That is the kind of perspective I gained from examining the roles my parents played in their lives and how those cultural norms affected me.

I am extremely grateful that I had so many years to develop in my relationship with them and to heal much of the painful parts. As I established a healthier identity for myself apart from them, I was able to be with them more comfortably. They were both wonderful grandparents and made themselves available to help with both my children any time I needed them. That helped me develop a new and deeper appreciation of who they were as people.

Some old barriers were broken down when they became grandparents and again when they became great-grandparents. Kaya named my father JoJo when she was about a year old. Immediately, the whole family began to call him that, and it felt like his nickname lightened up all our connections. And then, à la Kaya, we all called my mother by her first name, Amy. The dynamic in the whole family changed at that time. We all seemed to see them differently as "Amy and JoJo," and not just in the roles they had played as parents. I think we all bonded around Kaya and enjoyed having four generations together when we gathered for holidays or summer vacations.

My mother died three years after my father. I had always hoped she would have some time without him to experience herself more as a separate person, but she was already too infirm to redefine herself as an individual in the world without him. She did very well for herself, though: she kept her house up in a warm and welcoming way, had parts of the family over on many Sundays, saw a few friends, and enjoyed her TV shows as if they were her life. My son, Bill, got married and had a baby, Gigi, who was a great joy and became the center of my mother's emotional world. Gigi loved her and called her Amy.

When Amy died, Gigi was only three years old. Gigi used to look up at the sky and say, "We love you, Amy." It was an amazing connection, and Gigi seemed to intuitively know how to say good-bye to her great-grandmother, who had adored her.

After someone dies, it is natural to regret not being closer, appreciating them more when they were alive, or having more acceptance of them in the relationship. If you were distant with someone, there were probably some good reasons, and it is possible you have some unresolved issues with that person. Write about it—either as a journal entry or in a letter—now or when you are ready. If that is not enough, talk to a professional or someone you trust to help you sort it out more deeply.

Pause. Take Three Breaths. Consider: What were some of the cultural expectations or norms that affected your relationship with your parents? Were there some role-related reasons for the challenges in your relationship? How much of your identity was still connected to them? What do you wish you might have done differently, beyond the role you had with them? Has your identity changed being without them? In what ways? Is there a sense of freedom since they are gone? Write or talk about it.

Loss of a Child

We have the term *widow,* and we have the term *orphan,* but there is no word to describe the position of someone who has lost a child. Everyone seems to agree that losing a child is the worst loss of all. We are not meant to bury an offspring. It is unnatural and out of the basic order of life and death. Losing an offspring is never easy. I feel worst for parents who lose a very young child with all the potential and time together that feels taken away.

If a child of yours has died, no matter how old he or she was, you are likely to be in pain for quite a while, including feelings about the role you played as your child's parent. It is the parent's job to keep a child alive, so one often feels like a failure on many levels if the child dies before the parent.

Today I am extremely grateful for my role as Chris's mother for thirty-two years. She was a beautiful child with a sweet heart. I remember carrying her in my belly and poking her there, and she'd punch back with a hand or foot; I couldn't tell which.

She and I were extremely close, and I would say now that I over-identified with her in a major way. I also know now that I put some of my unmet emotional needs from my first marriage onto my little daughter. With my son, Bill, I was a little more distant and one might say more appropriate. I had boundaries with him that were nonexistent with Chris. She was my heart, and I know in hindsight that I put that burden on her. Even though it was a fraught relationship, I loved her dearly.

Of course, she did not feel like a blessing in my life when she was sneaking into my house against my will and using drugs, or when she was driving drunk with Kaya. I totally did not appreciate having to go to court to take her daughter away from her to protect Kaya from her mother's inappropriate behavior.

I had to examine every part of my relationship with her after she died. I had to look at the ways that, as much as I had loved my children, I had been self-centered and self-absorbed as a mother and not attuned to either of them. It's a burning pain to face the deficiencies one had as a parent after your child has died. It's hard not to feel like a failure. Sometimes it's even hard not to feel like you killed your child or contributed to his or her death in some major way.

My grief at Chris's death was especially ruthless, and I had to ruthlessly look at all the parts of that relationship. Even before she died, I grieved each time I lost a bit of her to her disease—no high school diploma, no career path, and, at times, no home. But the finality of her death put me into the deepest pain I had ever experienced. Examining the role I was in as her mother when she died was another way of processing the relationship and coming to terms with her interrupted life and her early, self-destructive end.

Offspring die in many different ways. How it happened becomes less important over time, and what abides is an emptiness that cannot be completely filled. I find that I have a tendency to "adopt" young women of my daughter's generation. It is part of my recovery from losing her, and has been mutually beneficial to me and I'm pretty sure to my younger female friends. No one replaces anyone in our lives, but the roles can be filled in many creative ways. I get to experience myself in similar relationships, and I have found it to be healing to my sense of self.

Pause. Take Three Breaths. Consider: If you have lost an offspring, how responsible do you feel about his or her death? Can you see that it wasn't your fault? Although this kind of loss is one of the most difficult aspects of life to accept, can you imagine that you could come to accept that your child is gone from this planet and has left his or her body? Do you have any relationships in your life that let you play the role of nurturing adult? Would you want to experience that more? Write or talk about it.

Loss of a Sibling

My son, Bill, said that when his only sibling, Chris, died, he lost the witness to his childhood. When we were writing together, he even wrote a section called "No Witnesses," in which he described the loss of his constant childhood companion and what it feels like to be missing that person to check in with about memories and significant events.

Bill also talked a lot about what it felt like to "become an only child." I think he felt some pressure from that role—like he was all his father and I had now, and that gave him an increased sense of responsibility to the family and maybe even in the world.

One of the most painful aspects of losing a sibling is related to sibling rivalry. The natural rivalry between siblings to get their needs met in the family is intensified when the resources are limited, either physically or emotionally. When one sibling doesn't survive, the surviving siblings are prone to feeling some major guilt for surviving. Giving yourself permission to be alive when your sibling is not can feel very primal and involve intense survivor guilt.

Another difficult feeling to allow for after a sibling dies is relief. If there weren't enough resources to fulfill each offspring's needs in the family, a certain relief can follow when one of them dies. "I don't have to compete anymore," or even, "I'm glad they are gone" are parts of ruthless grief.

There are also many families in which the siblings are quite distant or even alienated from one another. In these cases, when one of the siblings dies there is often very little feeling about the loss, but there can be guilt about the lack of emotional response. "Maybe I should be feeling more about my sister's death; I mostly feel nothing about it because we weren't close at all." This is an example of the need to give yourself permission to have all your feelings in your emotional work of grieving. In my practice, I have noticed that sometimes the siblings' relationship matches that of the parents. For example, if the parents were very alienated from or hostile to each other, the siblings tend to echo the same dynamic. This can also be a source of guilt when a sibling dies until the survivor realizes they were just repeating their parents' patterns of relationship.

The change in the family dynamic when a sibling dies is often huge. I have heard so many stories of people feeling like they have also lost a parent when their sibling dies because of the way the parent is stuck or lost in grief for his or her offspring. I was very aware of this risk with my son and made extra efforts to be with him and available for his feelings after his sister died.

Bob's oldest brother died of lung cancer in his thirties. The siblings were very close, and Bob was deeply affected by his death. I know he stopped smoking right after John died and never smoked again. He also talked about the profound effect his brother's death had on his mother. He felt like he had lost both his mother and his brother because of her subsequent collapse into her pain.

Bob told me that he and his remaining siblings finally wrote their mother a letter about a year after their brother died: "Ma, we need you. Johnny is gone, but you have three more surviving kids who miss their mother. Please come back." This note had a profound effect on Bob's mother. She began to return to the living, emerging from under her dark cloud of grief.

In Chapter 8, I wrote about my friend Fran, and the profound effect her brother's suicide had on the rest of her life, until she could begin to face the feelings that were buried with him. We tend to define ourselves by the relationships in our family of origin, and when those shift, our sense of who we are can change.

Pause. Take Three Breaths. Consider: How close were you to your sibling? How strong was your sibling rivalry? How have the dynamics in your family changed since his or her death? Do you have any regrets about your relationship with your sibling?

Loss of a Friend

The death of a close friend is very personal and often causes us to look at how we are living our own lives and how we will eventually die. When a friend dies, it feels like a part of us and our history goes too. It breaks an attachment that was not family but was quite important to our life and to our identity. Of course, there are instances where a friendship is much closer than family.

This past summer I lost a close friend to death for the first time. I admired and loved Nancy for her unique person and our unique connection. Of course I had lost many friends before, as a result of geographical changes or drifting apart, but the loss to a death felt very different. The interruption aspect was strong, and the need to face my own mortality confronted me powerfully. We were the exact same age, born a day apart. We used to say we were twins separated at birth.

Actually, we could not have been more different. She was from Puerto Rico and was single for many years with no children. During her very brief marriage, she had a son who was stillborn. There was a part of her that never recovered from that loss, but it also gave her what I would call a soulful depth, even a mysterious quality, that drew me to her. She was highly empathic and sensitive to the feelings of others. When she left, there was a hole in my life and the lives of her other friends. We gathered more often for a time, remembering her and telling stories about our time with her. We discovered that we each knew different aspects of her, and we learned how different each of our friendships with her had been.

Nancy was a natural poet and writer who did not take her gift for writing seriously. She would write out little ditties on scraps of paper and humbly read them at occasions like birthdays or anniversaries. Sadly, much of her writing couldn't be found after her death. That loss had a profound effect on me and has emboldened me to take my own writing more seriously and to fulfill the writer in me with more consciousness. Thank you, Nancy.

I recently went to the memorial of an old friend with whom I had lost contact for the last ten years of our lives. She was eighty-two when she died. At the memorial I learned about the many interesting things she had done in her final decade: cruises to the Mediterranean, falling in love with Turkey, and her intense spiritual search in reading and conversation with friends. I felt the loss of my connection with her and felt inspired to reach out to friends more regularly; I want to appreciate those who are left in my life and not take any friendships for granted.

Pause. Take Three Breaths. Consider: What friends have you lost to death? How close were you? What regrets did you have? How did you identify with them? Did you learn anything from their passings? Do you have friends who are still alive who you want to reach out to more? Make a list, and make time to call them.

SHIFTING IDENTITY

As you have moved through your emotional work about losing your loved one, and you've examined the role or roles he or she played in your life, you have probably experienced shifting feelings about who you are in the world. At times after my profound losses, I could feel my identity changing, and I didn't completely recognize who I was becoming. I had heavily identified myself as a mother and wife, and suddenly I was a single woman in the world and the mother of only a son. I did lean heavily on the role of grandmother, and I needed that role in life to bolster my sense of self (and still do). I am also a clinical psychologist with a successful private practice, and that role has helped me throughout my adult life.

However, there is a part of each of us that transcends all the details of our lives and all the roles we play with others. Some would call it our essence or our soul. It is the part of me that I experience when I am at the ocean or listening to music. It is the part of me that I contact when I meditate or pray, look up at the sky, or walk in the woods. In ruthless grief, we have the opportunity to contact that aspect of ourselves, because something essential has been stripped away and we are forced to look at the more core aspects of having the gift of a human life. I look up at the sky often and experience being alive in the world apart from all the details of my life.

As you move ruthlessly through the grieving process, you can develop a sense of self that transcends all the roles in your life and come to an experience of your more essential self. Since my losses, which have also included the deaths of both my parents within the last several years, I have come to a sense of myself in the world as a loving human being, beyond the expectations of culture and kin.

My permission to be alive has become permission to be myself no matter what. It is a sense of having more freedom and choices in life beyond the roles I played as wife, mother, and daughter. At the same time, my identity or sense of self in the roles I still play started to feel less constricting and less tied to the expectations of how I "should" behave with my loved ones.

In the next section we will examine what comes next, how we experience ourselves without our loved ones and the roles we played with them in our lives. Permission to be alive becomes permission to go on without them and to become ourselves in new and creative ways. After some time and energy, that permission has become an affirmation of my life force as myself. It also became a permission to love them and myself even more freely. In ruthless grief, we hope to accept this loss, and beyond that acceptance, to achieve a sense of self that transcends the losses we have experienced.

THINGS TO REMEMBER

- Looking at the role you played with your lost loved one can provide you with an important perspective on understanding the relationship as it related to culturally defined norms and how you experienced yourself within those norms.

- Be aware of your feelings about the role you played and how you played it. Look at how compatible that role was for you, how creative or constricted you felt in it, and how well suited you were to it.

- Allow that you and your loved one are flawed humans in those defined roles. Write down the plusses and minuses of the cultural norms and how they suited you.

- Consider any deeper resentments or mistakes that need to be addressed.

- Continue to write letters to your loved one or in your journal to help resolve any leftover resentments or lingering guilt.

- Acknowledge all your efforts with your loved one and consider that there were probably reasons for some of the flaws in both of you and in your relationship as a whole.

- Give some thought (including meditation and prayer) to who you are beyond the role you were in with your loved one. Consider the parts of your identity that transcend any details of your life—like how you experience yourself in nature (being near water or looking up at the sky) or listening to music.

- Be available for aspects of your identity to shift as you let go more deeply.

PART THREE

Going On
Without Them

CHAPTER 10

The Magic of Acceptance: Nurturing Your Creative Imagination

Acceptance is a theme throughout this book. It's important to know we cannot force ourselves into acceptance, but we are heading toward it on our journey of grief. It begins when we give ourselves permission to be alive. If we practice this on a daily basis, we will have glimpses of acceptance that occur even early in loss.

The process continues with accepting our feelings, no matter what they are or are not. Feeling numb is often hard to accept. Feeling relieved is also challenging to feel and often occurs in any grief process at some time. Anger is often a troublesome emotion and is especially challenging to deal with in loss. We cannot do our grief work without accepting that we have our feelings and need to express them. That is why the concept of Permission is such an important part of grieving. Acceptance of feeling numb, feeling anger, feeling lost without our loved one, or feeling whatever it is we are feeling at any given time is crucial for moving through the grieving process so we can proceed with our lives in the healthiest way possible.

Permission to feel what you feel is key. We have done a lot of emotional work to accept and allow ourselves to have all of our feelings, no matter how painful. We have learned to ride the waves of our grief and to know and experience that they pass, as waves do.

Acceptance can also come in waves. At first it is just a ripple, a glimmer of accepting this loss as part of your life experience. It is the opposite of the waves of grief, which begin big and are sometimes a tsunami of pain and loss. The waves of acceptance start small and gradually increase over time.

RUTHLESSNESS OF ACCEPTANCE

In the beginning, the idea of accepting that our loved ones are gone and how they left can feel a little ruthless. It feels disloyal, as if we would forget them if we accept that they have left their bodies. "This I will never accept" could be an attitude that comes up early in loss and can persist and keep us stuck in grief and pain. I have been gently leading you through the process toward acceptance—of your loved ones, of how they left, of your relationship with them, and of yourself throughout your grief and beyond toward the goal of reinvesting in life without them.

Acceptance isn't something you can decide to do. Willingness is the key. You can become willing to accept this loss and then let nature take its course. The death of someone close is never easy to accept. Acceptance seems to come unbidden after you've done your emotional work, dealt with your anger, obsessed about your loved one however much you need to, shed your tears, faced the sadness without medicating, and acknowledged, not avoided, your deepest feelings.

Acceptance of Distorted Thinking

You need to be very aware of what you are thinking in your grief. We covered a lot of this in Chapter 6 Obsessions: What-Ifs and Regrets, about accepting how obsessive grief can be and giving yourself permission to be in your obsessive thoughts for a time. What you need to work on changing and not accepting is some of your thinking during grief—your grief thoughts, which are often fear or even self-hating thoughts.

As we have said, thoughts shortly after loss tend to be very negative and feed your low self-esteem. Some of the depressive thoughts we faced and faced down include "I didn't deserve them in my life, anyway." "I am being punished for something I did a long time ago." "I should just die, too." It can be a tricky balance to be aware of your distorted thinking, to accept that you are in it for a time, and then to find another, more positive perspective to honor your loved one and yourself in a more positive light. Accepting your negative, grief-stricken thinking as the truth can be destructive and dangerous. Instead, accept that you will engage in such thinking sometimes.

Pause. Take Three Breaths. Consider: Have you entertained any distorted thoughts during your grief that still persist about your loved one? About yourself? Can you find another perspective with more compassion on how you see yourself and the person you lost?

Perfectionism

We are all flawed humans, and nothing brings up those flaws more than grief. I recently heard a woman crying about how much she took for granted having her father in her life and not appreciating him until after he died; this is a very human and common feeling.

One thing that interferes majorly with acceptance is perfectionism. In fact, it can interfere with many aspects of grieving, including emotional upheaval. Emotions are messy and perfectionism does not allow that in any way. Perfectionism is something you have to be ruthless about to push through this habit of thought and behavior.

You might have been confronting your perfectionism at every turn when you've had a loss. It isn't unusual to be asking yourself things like, "How can I accept such an imperfect, and sometimes chaotic, process? I feel so lost; I've made so many mistakes with my loved one. How can I be messy or all over the place emotionally?"

The book *Addiction to Perfection* recounts in detail how destructive and pervasive perfectionism can be. It describes perfectionism as a compulsion of thought and behavior that can color our entire experience of living and interfere with the positive experiences of life. It can get us off our own side and keep us in our grief longer and more painfully than might be necessary.

Pause. Take Three Breaths. Consider: How perfectionistic have you generally been in your life? How much has it affected your grieving? How forgiving can you be toward yourself? Toward your loved one who left?

We will talk about forgiveness in Chapter 11. However, acceptance and forgiveness do go well together. Moreover, a forgiving attitude toward yourself and others is the key to intervening on the habit of being a perfectionist.

We have faced the many different ways we try to control the grieving process. It is a process that requires vulnerability to get through. Our egos feel strong when we think we are in charge, but ruthless grieving requires the strength of being vulnerable. I learned early on in my own growth that my strength is in my vulnerability, even though it hardly ever feels like that. In her book, *The Gifts of Imperfection: Let Go of Who You Think You're Supposed to Be and Focus on Who You Are,* Brene Brown writes about the challenges and strengths of being vulnerable in all areas of life. Embracing the imperfection of being human and giving up control are part of the paradox of ruthless grief.

Don't Fight the Traffic

Acceptance is a frequent topic of conversation in therapeutic and spiritual circles. Deepak Chopra writes in his *Seven Spiritual Laws of Success* that anything we resist will persist. He writes, "If you are fighting with the traffic, you are fighting with the forces of the entire universe." I learned from that book how *not* to fight the traffic—nor with anything that happens—most of the time.

I deal pretty well with physical traffic now. I tell myself, "It's okay that I am sitting in this traffic; I can look around, turn on better music, or make a call on speaker." However, if it goes on too long for me, I can still lose it sometimes and get agitated. "This should not be happening. I hate to be late. Where did all these cars come from? They should go home." It's an ongoing process, and I am still working on it. I spend a lot of time in my car since I live and work in two different locations about one hundred miles apart, so I still have lots of opportunities for practice.

Of course *don't fight the traffic* is also a metaphor, and it has been a powerful one for me. I learned this principle before Bob and Chris died, but I had to practice the idea of it frequently after they left. I think glimmers of it started early as I practiced my permission to be alive. The words, "It's okay that I am alive and they are not" would seem to contain full acceptance, but acceptance of their deaths was a very gradual process. That is why I have written about "Permission to be Alive" in each of the three sections of this book. The nature of the permission changes and deepens as we practice it on a daily basis, the same way any spiritual or emotional practice changes and grows within us over time.

Radical Acceptance

Another popular aspect of acceptance comes from the area of cognitive therapy, which works primarily with the ways we think. There is a popular term now called Radical Acceptance. It is part of a cognitive approach called dialectical behavior therapy (DBT). In Radical Acceptance, we are encouraged to work on approaching everything in life with acceptance. I learned acceptance from Deepak Chopra, but Radical Acceptance is the same essential way of thinking. A friend of mine uses the affirmation, "Allow what is to be." Those are powerful words, and they now comfort me when I think of Bob and Chris.

Equal Moments

I have heard that an exalted spiritual goal is for every moment to be equal to every other moment in our lives—not to play favorites. Of course, the present moment is always the one we want to "favor." I pick this moment. It is picking me, so I might as well pick it back. Welcome the ever new and ever-changing moment.

Life never stands still, and resisting it is never comfortable, though very human and natural. It is the illusion of control that fuels our resistance. "No" is one of the first words we utter, and refusal is a necessary part of life and also an inevitable part of grief. In dealing with loss, this resistance needs to change over time. "No" eventually turns into a surrender to what is, in an organic and subtle way. In surrender, we find some peace of mind.

Giving ourselves "Permission to be Alive" can broaden and deepen as we practice it. "This moment is okay, even though I have lost this person to death. I am not dead, and I'm willing to be grateful for that" is a huge step in that direction.

Interrupted but Complete

The gift of a human life is a miraculous thing. We have faced that gift being taken away, in a specific human form, and we have not liked it. Death is the rapacious creditor, and we have to learn to accept its realities. Again, I found that I had to find the ruthless part of myself to reach acceptance of Bob and Chris's deaths and my losses surrounding them. There is also a fierceness in accepting everything life has to offer, even the pain and loss that are part of it. This requires courage, even though acceptance seems like a more passive stance in life. It definitely is not. It is active and courageous. Acceptance is vulnerability and allows us to let go of control, which helps the healing process.

> **Pause. Take Three Breaths. Consider:** What are some of the aspects of this loss that have been the most difficult to accept? What is still in your way of full acceptance? How courageous or fierce do you feel in moving toward acceptance? Do you even believe that acceptance is an option?

When I asked myself those questions early on, I came up with several obstacles. For me, one of the most difficult things to accept was that Bob's and Chris's lives were both interrupted, that they didn't get the natural progression of a life into older age. I also had trouble accepting that I didn't get to progress with each of them into those stages of human life. I don't get to grow old with the man I loved the most. On our first Christmas together, I gave Bob a mug with a sketch John Lennon made for Yoko Ono that said, "Grow Old with Me"—not happening. And, of course, I don't get to be the mother of a mature and older daughter.

Bob was just beginning to enjoy his new career as a therapist. Chris missed out on seeing her daughters grow up and on helping them to do that. I wasn't complete with either one of them, but mostly I couldn't accept that it felt like *they* were incomplete.

I came to believe that they must have been complete—that they had to be. They were *done*. I still have trouble believing that at times, but I think it is true. I still have occasional waves of sadness, some deep, about their shortened lives, but most of the time, I don't fight the traffic. I came to believe that Bob and Chris were complete and I was not. I had to find ways to complete the relationships for myself. This whole process is one of learning to complete what was not complete for us. In writing letters to our loved ones or to God, in communing with nature, in observing rituals we created and shared, in having the courage to experience the depth of all our painful feelings, we have come to acceptance of life without them.

One other aspect of coming to some completion and acceptance is developing our creative imagination about the person we lost, putting together our concepts of where he is and what she might be "doing."

CREATIVE IMAGINATION

Your creative imagination can take you closer to a full acceptance of loss. We have touched on the concept of creative imagination throughout the book, but I want to spell out for you some of the creative ideas I have developed to avoid torturing myself with my losses.

Recently, I read a book called *Proof of Heaven* by Evan Alexander, in which he recounts an intense near-death experience he had during a serious illness. His experience was very beautiful, and when he came back he realized he had seen things that he could not have just conjured up.

I personally have come to believe in a paradise, and I do believe that the people I have known who have passed are there. Why not believe that? Whether it is true or not, we cannot go wrong imagining that our loved ones are in the best place for them and that they are very much not suffering.

The author describes going through a very dark place and feeling like an earthworm, but knowing beyond words that he was loved and totally belonged. There were no words, but he knew there were no mistakes in life, and everything happened the way it was meant to. That was followed by a magical experience of light and beauty filled with an amazing phenomenon of colorful images and experiences.

That book helped me enormously this year. I guess I was ready for it. It helped me to relax even more deeply into the safety and comfort of the Other Side. It even helped me to feel so much better about the prospect of my own death. Whether it is creative imagination or true contact with a spiritual dimension has become less important to me. I have resigned from the debating society and have accepted other realities in my life. That process started with reading the book *The Lovely Bones* in the fall of 2001, after Bob and Chris had gone.

Previously, all I knew was that it was about a little girl who had died. It turned out to be a great read written in the voice of the little girl from "her heaven." It describes where she was, in a beautiful gazebo, enjoying all the things she loved and occasionally looking down on her loved ones and sending them good energy. She would feel a "pinch" when they were feeling pain about her death, and she would wish them well.

That was when I began to use my own creative imagination to picture Bob and Chris in "their heaven." I sometimes pictured them together, but I'm pretty sure they would not have been a big part of each other's paradise. I imagine that Chris's is similar to the little girl's in *The Lovely Bones,* and she is surrounded by children and animals, except her paradise played rock and roll music, including lots of Grateful Dead and Joni Mitchell.

I recently watched a special on PBS about the Grateful Dead and felt that I had a little visit with Chris. I felt warm and loving about the experience of the music and felt close to her. Even though it wasn't my favorite music, it was hers for many years, and I felt her lovely, loving spirit coming through the lilting, repetitive tunes.

Bob's heaven, as I imagined it, was different. Bob would have the Hollywood version of heaven. He was an actor who loved live theater. Bob is doing theater in his paradise and getting lots of attention and praise for it. He is playing with talented souls and loving it.

This is the kind of constructive imagination that comforted and soothed me through my grief. There is no reason not to try it, and your envisioned paradise might even be true. If not, you are still more accepting and at peace than you would be without your imaginative, creative efforts. I personally believe in my experiences of the spiritual dimension, and I encourage you to develop your own. You might be surprised by where they take you.

We will now pick up on our progressive ideas about giving yourself permission for living on without them. In my experience, this permission gains in depth as we practice it and becomes an important part of a way of being, one that has brought me much satisfaction and even a deeper joy of living than I had ever experienced before.

Permission to Be Alive

The most advanced practice of "Permission to be Alive," which moves your journey toward acceptance, is embracing all of life fully. It is the highest expression of gratitude. "I am simply grateful to be alive and accept my life as it is." This more grateful permission to be alive is not about any specific aspect of life. It is about coming to a place where you are grateful for *every* aspect of life, even the challenges . . . sometimes especially the challenges.

In the beginning of grief, you just need a simple permission to be alive today—accepting that you are alive and breathing without your loved one—accepting your life force in this moment. You often don't want to, but you practice deciding to accept being alive anyway. The first week after Bob's death, when I visited my friend Susan and lay on her healing table, I had that first permission to be alive in my body and my first glimmer of acceptance.

Through the emotional work you've done, you learned to accept your feelings about your departed loved one and about how your life had been with him or her and how it was now that he or she is gone. These are the concepts we covered in the second permission—permission to have your emotional process and every part of it.

Now that permission takes a giant leap and progresses to a feeling of acceptance of everything. As I came to accept Bob's and

Chris's deaths, I began to accept everything that happened in a day and found that I was more accepting of most people as well. I also became more accepting of myself than I had ever been.

Gratitude

My practice of gratitude began long before 2001. I learned it in my 12-Step meetings, and it helped me enormously when I was grieving my divorce and dealing with my troubled teenagers. Gratitude was actually a key to my personal recovery and had changed me a great deal before Bob and Chris died.

A book by Sarah Ban Breathnach titled *Simple Abundance* also contributed to this attitude. She suggests writing down five moments that you are grateful for at the end of every day. For me, choosing specific times in the day made my gratitude more real and less conceptual. "I am grateful to be healthy" turned into, "I felt so satisfied with my body during that yoga class." I started doing that in the 90s and found many benefits from the practice. I also found that as the practice developed in me, I didn't want to stop at five moments and went on to at least ten most days.

In grief, gratitude is often the last thing one wants to approach, and it certainly doesn't come unbidden, unless the relationship was horrendous. If the person who has died was extremely troublesome to you, it is totally natural to feel grateful he or she is gone. Permission to be alive starts the glimmers of acceptance and of gratitude. However, saying "Thank you for this loss" is not where most of us begin. Gratitude develops over time as we go through our mourning.

I did feel grateful that neither Bob nor Chris had suffered too much in their dying. Bob had experienced a lot of pain during his last month, but we had hospice workers in our house, he was medicated appropriately for the most part, and the care was great. That was one of the first things I was able to feel gratitude about: that he wasn't suffering now, and that there had been amazing people who supported us through his dying and after.

After Chris's death, I couldn't feel gratitude for many months. The first gratitude I felt was that she would not live her life for many years as a heroin addict on the streets, suffering the pains of addiction and being alienated from her two girls while she was still on the planet. Cold comfort, at first, that grew into a genuine gratitude that she didn't have to suffer longer.

"Shit happens," and this happened in my life. I can't fight the traffic anymore. What's the point? I accepted it, and it turned into gratitude for all of life's experiences.

Acceptance in Fast Forward

I had something happen recently that I found very difficult to accept. I was responsible for it happening, and I was certainly guilty of being careless and preoccupied, which made it harder to accept. It was a loss of material objects that typified for me all the stages of grieving.

I had just returned from a week visiting China and Kaya in Los Angeles. I had been back in New York City for three days, working and seeing clients, and I hadn't unpacked my suitcase. I still had all my favorite clothes packed from the trip and had also put my computer in the side pocket to take to Sag Harbor, which I really consider home. I had several other packages with me: a separate laundry bag, my large purse with books and current necessities, and a bag of groceries.

I was double-parked by a fire hydrant as I packed up my car. I had already put my dog into the car and, I acknowledged a woman in a wheelchair who came out of my building as I packed up the car. When I'd finished, I pulled away from the curb and happily drove off to Sag Harbor.

When I arrived, I noticed that my suitcase was not in the back seat. I looked in the trunk—not there. Gradually I realized that I had not put my suitcase in the car. I had left it on the street in New York City, right in front of my apartment building.

I panicked. The suitcase had all my favorite clothes, and, most important, my beloved computer. I realized in the next few hours how attached I am to my computer, much more than to my favorite outfits. It also had nine chapters of this book in it.

I went through all the stages of grief. I was in shock, and every few hours I would realize what had happened, and my whole body would cringe. I thoroughly believed that I would get everything back—that was my denial that it was gone. I called my dog walker and asked him to put a note with my phone number in my lobby for people to watch for it and return it to me. I was so sure it would be returned.

That belief was interspersed with blaming myself bitterly for my big mistake. I kept going back to the moment of getting in the car and wishing I'd remembered the bag on the street. I kept thinking, "You just threw all your stuff away, just put it in the garbage." My friend Susan was visiting me for the weekend, and I kept talking to her about it and was obsessive about blaming myself and regretting the moment I had lost it.

Over the course of the next few days, as no one called with information, I began to accept that I had lost my suitcase. I was pretty sure that my editor had copies of almost everything from the book, but I felt lost without my computer. A friend suggested that I could tell my insurance company that my bag had been stolen from my car. I entertained that idea for about twelve hours. That exercise led me to write down all the items that were in the bag and even the dollar amounts of what the contents were worth. I woke up the next morning knowing that I couldn't lie about losing it, which helped me to further accept that it was gone.

When I got back to New York City on Sunday evening, the suitcase was sitting in my lobby. I was thrilled at the sight of it. *Life is good,* I thought. *New Yorkers are honest, all is right with the world, there is a God.* Those were my thoughts until I got to the bag and found that all the contents were gone. In fact, it was full of two bags of garbage. My hopes were dashed.

Seeing the empty suitcase reminded me of that period of searching and yearning, where you think you see your deceased loved one on the street. It reminded me of searching for Bob's mustard color winter jacket or Chris's dreadlocks and thinking for a moment that they were there. My bag was there, but the valued contents were gone.

For about a week, as I had done with Bob and Chris, I searched my street, looking for an item of my clothing or my computer with the little smiley-face sticker on the front. I asked Billy, the homeless man on my block who I had never spoken to before, if he'd seen anything. He had not.

It took me a week to buy myself a new computer. I had to adjust for several days to the fact that the last one was gone.

I write this not to trivialize any of our human losses, but to describe, in fast forward, the process of grief over any loss—the self-recrimination, the denial, the hope of return, the surrender, and the acceptance.

It's a lot easier to accept losing clothes and a computer than to accept losing a loved one. Part of this process involves the deepest mystery of existence as a human. We go to the deep philosophical questions: "Why do people die?" "Why did they go in that particular way?" "Why am I alive when they are not?" "Why am I living?"

Pause. Take Three Breaths. Consider: What questions are still with you about this mystery? Where do you believe they are? Is there a way that you picture them? Have you fully accepted all that happened? What philosophical questions remain for you?

Moving toward the acceptance of significant loss as I do my emotional and spiritual work, I experience acceptance of myself and others. "Allow what is to be" has to include me. I have gotten to know myself so much more as I have gone through all the phases of loss. As I have learned to accept Bob and Chris, how they lived and died, and how their loss has affected me, self-acceptance has crept in, and it seems to stay.

Getting Over It

Some people say we never get over the loss of someone near and dear to us. I think that expression suggests the wrong premise. We get through all the effects of the loss and we emerge, changed in the deepest ways we know. "I will never be the same" is very different from "I'll never get over it." In her book *On Grief and Grieving*, Elisabeth Kübler-Ross writes, "The reality is you will grieve forever. You will not 'get over' the loss of a loved one: you will learn to live with it. You will heal and you will rebuild yourself around the loss you have suffered. You will be whole again but you will never be the same. Nor should you be the same, nor would you want to."

My experience is we don't grieve forever. Yes, waves of grief will always be some part of your experience. However, I emphasize that the bulk of your healing work is something to "get through" not "get over," and you *can* get through it.

We come out the other side of grief changed, transformed into more of who we truly are. Grief takes a hold of you and shakes all the "not you" from you, and what is left is so much closer to who you really are. So you shouldn't want to be the same, and you are not, but in so many ways you have a chance to become more whole and more deeply yourself.

I'm reminded of the third act of the classic play *Our Town*. In it, the deceased are portrayed as people sitting in individual chairs, but they give the impression of tombstones. Mourners visit them and writhe on the ground in pain about the loss of their loved ones. The dead "chair" people turn to each other and say, "They just don't get it, do they?"

194

We often don't "get it" for a long while, and then we do. What I got was that death is just a part of life. The dead aren't suffering, and they don't want us to suffer either. We do for a while, and then when we fully accept they are gone and needed to go, we don't suffer anymore.

THINGS TO REMEMBER

- Acceptance cannot be willed, but it can be taken as a goal of grief.

- The daily practice of "Permission to Be Alive" is where we start, and it begins the journey toward acceptance.

- Acceptance comes in waves. It starts as a glimmer and gradually increases to a place of acceptance and peace of mind.

- The practice of acceptance is a high spiritual goal and applies to everything in life. "Allow what is to be."

- As we practice acceptance of this loss and how it affects us, a deep acceptance of self can emerge.

- "Permission to Be Alive" develops into gratitude and can nurture and transform us in our journey toward acceptance and beyond to a full, rich life.

CHAPTER 11

All That's Left: Tools for Living

Our entire process has been one of self-examination and the development of compassion for ourselves and others. These are the most effective tools for living a healthy life, and we have had to develop (or at least hone) them to get through our grief in a conscious and compassionate manner.

As the depth of my grief subsided, I found that I was more present to my life than I had ever been before. My consciousness had been changed. It's a long journey from the shock and awe we had in the beginning, although the awe of early grieving was the beginning of my shift in consciousness. The permission to be alive today was a big part of that change. I had practiced living one day at a time for years before my losses, but with the pain of loss, my sense of the day and of being alive in it deepened when it shifted to "Permission to be alive, today, when they are not." That and the appreciation of just being alive grew deeper as I went through the stages of my losses.

ALL THAT IS LEFT

It is my experience of grief that when the core of our work is complete, all that is left is the love. I feel only love for Bob and Chris. Nothing else is left. In *Harry Potter and the Deathly Hallows*, Dumbledore says that grief *is* love. There are so many other places we

196

go with grief, but, in the end, we hopefully land on love as a final destination.

Resentment and Forgiveness

When we look at what is left after we've worked through our grief, we have to speak of resentment and forgiveness. I know people who are still carrying around resentments with people who are long dead. They are gone, but the resentments are still alive and well.

Resentment

Now, if there were many destructive aspects in your life with the person who is gone, or if, as we've mentioned at other times in this book, this person was a damaging person in your life, I don't want to set up the expectation of "All that is left is the love." Permission to have your feelings may not change all the resentments you might have toward that person, even though you've gone through all the stages of grieving him or her.

Pause. Take Three Breaths. Consider: Are there deep resentments left in you about the person who is gone? What are they? It might help to write them down. Would you consider forgiving that person?

You might answer no to the last question. I have dealt with many clients whose parents were so abusive and destructive to them that even after the parents died, forgiveness did not seem like an option. And sometimes it just isn't. What we want is peace of mind and serenity, and in some relationships those can be hard to come by.

Forgiveness

Let's talk about forgiveness. We forgive for ourselves, not for them. That could not be clearer when it comes to forgiving those who have died. They are fine, and we are the ones who might still be suffering.

Like acceptance, forgiveness is another "hard-work miracle" (see Chapter 9) that cannot be forced. We work and work and then it happens, but we cannot determine where or when, or even "if." I've noticed when I lead a group about forgiveness, the topic usually switches to anger. Of course, we might have some unresolved anger toward them and what happened to us with them.

Sometimes the best we can do is to forgive ourselves for still having negative feelings about the person who is gone. Accepting and forgiving yourself, even "siding with yourself" can be your key. In this case, treat resentment like regret: learn to just not give it much energy.

What you resist persists, so my suggestion is to accept that you still have some unresolved feelings about the deceased, including anger and resentments, and then cut off your energy to or about those feelings. Everything does not always get resolved. Life is not a Hollywood movie. Sometimes we need to live with some regret. Just don't give it a lot of energy by thinking about it, and let your regret wither and die a natural death, like a tumor where the blood supply is removed. If some pain lingers after you've done your work, don't let it fester.

For me, as with *je ne regrette rien* (I regret nothing), I still don't fully accept that I was a drug-addicted mother. I just don't fully accept it. My regret of being addicted to marijuana and how it affected my children is still present in me. However, except for writing about my regret in this book for the purpose of helping others, I don't give it energy, and it doesn't fester.

Unresolved Emotions

As a clinical psychologist, one of the emotional aspects I work on the most with clients is unresolved emotion. I frequently advise them to "Get it out," "Express it," and "Empty yourself of painful feelings."

However, in grieving, there are exceptions to this approach. Sometimes when we have gone through a conscious grief process and written or verbally expressed all our thoughts and feelings about the relationship, pockets of regret or resentment remain unresolved that don't always need expression.

Pause. Take Three Breaths. Consider: What is left of your resentments and regrets? If there are some, can you imagine just giving them less and less energy? What are the challenging feelings that still linger? Is forgiveness of yourself or the other person an option? Can you let those feelings die a natural death? Are you willing for that to happen in order to feel freer and more yourself?

In my experience, if you've worked on the tangle of hatred that can exist for some people in your life—whether they are alive or dead—and you've gotten on your own side about the mistakes you have made with them, then you can move ahead, focused on your self-acceptance and compassion for yourself, and the challenging feelings can die a natural death without taking you with them.

I reference the phrase from the Lord's Prayer: "Forgive us our trespasses, as we forgive those who trespass against us." In my experience, this is where willingness comes in. As I live in willingness to forgive others (even though I can't will it to happen), I am easier on myself, and often, miraculously the forgiveness comes.

Focus on What Remains

When I turn my attention to everything and everyone in my life, I experience a new appreciation for what and who is left with me. Truly, I can learn to focus on what is left, and it is almost always a lot.

I found that what was left was a wonderful life. I have work I love, an inner spiritual and creative life, nature all around me, a home that I used to share with my husband and that still has some of our loving energy in it with lots of fond memories.

There are endless ways to torture yourself, but by the time you've reached this point in the book, I hope you have mostly stopped. You have learned ways to work through your grief and (hopefully) are no longer torturing yourself with *what-ifs* and *if onlys*. If, when you've completed this book, you are aware of self-recrimination and major regrets, I suggest you go to a therapist or grief counselor for extra help.

I have a portrait that a friend painted of Bob and me and Kaya, when she was about six years old. We are at the little pond in front of our house, each staring into the water. It's a warm and personal, contemplative piece of art that hangs in my living room. It represents a very happy time in my life, when Bob and I were together building a life and spending a lot of time with our beloved eldest grand-daughter, whom we adored from the moment of her birth. Chris was still alive, living in Hawaii with China, but I don't focus on them when I look at that painting. Instead, I enjoy the happy memories of that time in my life.

I have also learned to focus on the people who are left in my life rather than on who is no longer there. I have a son, Bill, who is thriving in his life. He has a wife and two daughters who give me great joy. The littlest is Gigi, now ten, who is a spirited and beauti-ful child. I have two fully grown granddaughters, Chris's girls Kaya, twenty-four, and China, twenty. They both live in Los Angeles right now, but I am very close to them both.

I have a wonderful group of friends, about half of whom knew Bob and Chris. We talk about them sometimes, but not at all as much as we used to. I have a fun group of new friends and col-leagues who never knew me in my former life, and that works well for me also.

Metaphor of the Stuff

I recently spoke with an old friend whose husband died about a year before Bob. He had actually been a client of mine, and I wished that I had visited him when he was so ill. I remember I felt awkward as his therapist and, although Philadelphia was not that far from New York, the trip was an obstacle, as well.

He had been a painter and illustrator with some success. When he died, his wife, Victoria, put together a beautiful memorial of talks about him, interspersed with slides of his prolific art.

When I told Victoria about my experience of what happens in the long term after loss, and I said that all that is left is the love, she replied that she related to that, but her take on it was, "All that is left is the love and 500 paintings." Apparently, she has been daunted by what to do with all of her late husband's artwork and has just kept it hidden away in an expensive storage unit.

This brings up the question of what do we do with their stuff. Right after Bob died, I found that I enjoyed giving away his things and people were happy to receive them. I kept quite a few of his favorite shirts and wore them a lot in the beginning. I didn't have much left that had belonged to Chris, and I cherished her few possessions that were in my house. When someone is homeless, they don't have many possessions. I had some of the crafts she had made: some beaded jewelry, a few quilted pillows, and a necklace she had made for me with a photo of her in a small locket. Chris died the way she lived: not attached to much. What she left me were her two daughters, whom I have cherished the most in the fourteen years since she left.

In general, dealing with a departed loved one's things is part of the grieving process and can bring up some questions of attachment to objects and to the people who owned them. The question of what and how much to keep changes over time.

How we are with their belongings over the course of our grief and how we are with the emotional issues and attachments that are part of our grieving can be a metaphor for the grieving process itself. Early on, we often want to keep everything. Then as time goes by we find we want to keep just the essential items (sometimes very little). I found the same thing with my feelings. In the beginning, every aspect of the relationship and my feelings about it were very important. Then, as time passed, there was not that much that I needed to keep. Complex issues or feelings are the same; not that much of the baggage remains, just a few things. And then it reduces down to the care you had for each other and the love of them that persists . . . and a few sacred objects . . . and nurturing memories.

Creating a New Life Without Them

There are many spiritual principles or tools that have helped me "go on without them." I'd like to share some of them.

My joy of living comes from many sources. Basically it comes from within, as I have cleared the layers of defenses and ego that were crusted over my true self. I also embrace a belief from Zen Buddhism that a human life is a precious gift and very hard to come by. The chances of being born into a human life are very slim. I came to embrace these concepts more fully in living through the death of two of my closest humans.

I have also nurtured the "in" I have to the nonphysical world thanks to my losses, and I can enjoy my own Spirit more thoroughly. Partially, this is to honor them and what they would want for me and partially, it is coming to believe in and experiencing the true realities of living in the present—the precious gift of a human life. Their life was a gift to me, but my own life is the most precious gift of all.

Pause. Take Three Breaths. Consider: How connected do you feel to the joy of being alive as yourself? Are there moments when you feel it? What are those moments usually like, and where do they occur? Write them down regularly.

How can you experience more of them? Do you need to develop a spiritual practice to enhance them? Are you willing to explore that for yourself, if you haven't already?

Compassionate Joy

Then I am faced with the question of how do I live with others, when someone I loved the most has died? One of the best tools I found for this was the practice of compassionate joy. It is the attitude of being happy for other people's joy or good fortune. I learned it on a vacation in St. Croix, about nine months after Chris died.

I had become friendly with a recent widow in Sag Harbor, and she invited me to visit her in St. Croix in February. She was there for the winter, but she let me know a week before I was joining her that her thirty-five-year-old daughter would be joining us for the week. I felt panic and considered not going. I would be in this small cottage with a grown mother and daughter—it sounded too painful to bear. But I decided to go, mostly because I liked my friend and wanted to visit St. Croix in the winter.

Her daughter was very lovely and seemed quite open. On the first day we were out on a catamaran, and I remember she showed me her new bathing suit, a tankini, a two-piece bathing suit that covers your midsection—I loved it. My eyes filled with tears at the thought that my daughter would never be introducing me to new things or new ideas again. I thought about how Chris had taught me all about the environment and preserving it (when she worked for Greenpeace), and I cried some more.

On the catamaran that day in St. Croix, I decided to be happy for my friend, Barbara, who had this lovely grown daughter, even though I did not. It turned out Barbara was very worried about her daughter because she had just lost her job. I was able to help her put that into perspective. "My daughter just died, and you are going to color your whole time with yours about her unemployment?" I think she got it, but more important, *I* got that I could celebrate someone else's good fortune and not make it about me and my loss. People lose children in many different ways, and I lost mine—and life goes on. It's not all about me and my loss, and I can be happy for others who have what I no longer do.

Being truly happy for others in their triumphs and joys in life feels like an advanced way of being. Thinking or saying "I am very happy for you" creates a deep and transformative feeling when you can really mean it. Not comparing or despairing about others' happiness is a key to my satisfying life today.

I would often feel envy when I would see an older couple, even if they were just walking together on the street. My thought used to be, "How did they both stay alive?" I was surprised and a little astounded that some couples did get to grow old together. It felt amazing to me that this could occur. Of course it could, and does. Even my parents had that experience. My father lived to eighty-seven with my mother at his side to the end.

I learned to apply my compassionate joy to those sightings. "Good for them," I would tell myself. I also know that no relationship is completely ideal, and I remind myself that every couple has their own challenges and that living my single life has its benefits. It's a different take on compassionate joy, but it works for me if my envy gets too strong.

Practicing Gratitude

Another tool for living on without them is feeling satisfied with what we are experiencing—practicing gratitude. We have talked about the practice of noticing satisfying moments and writing them down. I like the word "practice" because we never get them completely, and using the term intervenes on any perfectionistic tendencies. I "practice" noticing satisfying moments, I "practice" gratitude, and I "practice" meditation and allowing what is to be.

I heard a spiritual talk recently about enjoying and taking in moments with loved ones. The speaker suggested cherishing the moments we have with the people we love. I thought about that as I considered friends who tend to measure the amount of time they get with their grown children and grandchildren. When I told a friend I thought it was great that she was able to see a grandson's performance at school and go out with the family afterward, her response was that she doesn't see them enough and that they are mostly too busy for her.

That is the opposite of cherishing the time we have with those we love. I am so fortunate to spend time with my son and his family. Those visits would be spoiled for me if I focused on how much I would like to see them more, or compared how much my other friends see their grandkids. I don't do it. My eldest granddaughters, Kaya and China, are both living in California. Right now, I get to see them every few months for a long weekend. I cherish those visits and enjoy my time with them.

I also have a brother and a son-in-law whom I cherish my time with. I sometimes have to work hard at not resenting how busy they are and how little I get to see them, but when I do spend some time with them, I thoroughly enjoy it.

I also cherish the time I have with my friends. There is a spiritual practice of greeting people as if you've never seen them before and then consciously parting as if you'll never see them again. I think the greeting used in yoga, *Namaste,* speaks to that: "The Spirit in me greets and honors the Spirit in you." While I don't think about these things all the time, they are healthy attitudes that I work at putting into practice.

205

What I Have Learned

Then there is what I have come to believe from my grieving. If life is all about learning, what have I learned?

I have learned that:

- Death is a part of life.

- Death happens in everyone's life, and it happened in mine.

- We all will die, so I value my life today more than ever.

- Love is the most important part of life.

- Everything in life is impermanent, so enjoy the moment.

- Accepting everything helps me not resist or resent whatever has occurred or is occurring in my life.

- I can accept myself and others.

- I still have some regrets, and I can live with them.

- Life is to be enjoyed, not endured nor suffered through.

I hope our journey together has reduced the negative baggage and let you focus positively on all that is left. We have focused on permissions, creative thinking, gratitude, and acceptance because those tools have helped me to establish a satisfying life, and I believe they are tools that will help you, too. We start with permission to be ruthless on our own behalf, and we complete the bulk of our grieving with acceptance and love. Truly, that is all that is left, and it is a lot.

THINGS TO REMEMBER

- We need to recognize on a daily basis the precious gift of having a human life.

- Our healing process starts with our practice of "Permission to Be Alive."

- Forgiveness of others and of ourselves is a gift to us, a "hard-work miracle" that can but does not always occur.

- Acceptance of any negative feelings or memories that are left can give us more peace of mind. Don't give energy to any negatives that are left.

- Compassionate joy helps us to live with others who have what we want or have lost.

- Resolving what to do with possessions left behind when our loved ones are gone is part of our grieving process and can help resolve our feelings about them in our lives and about "what is left."

- Focusing on our relationships with the people who are still with us is enlivening and nurturing.

- When the deepest part of our grief is complete, all that is left is the love.

CHAPTER 12

Helping Others Grieve: The Art of Presence

Grief can be transformative. This book is an emotional map about how to show up for the transformation and not get stuck in the myriad possibilities of boggy, rigid places. It can also be transformative and very moving to be close to someone who is grieving and to help them, in whatever way you can. Here is my best version of an emotional map for helping others grieve. I suggest that people grieving reach out to others—I found that helped me, while helping others at the same time. This chapter is also designed as a guide to supporting and assisting others when they are not personally in grief.

IDENTIFYING AND SHARING GRIEF

From the day I heard that Chris had died of an overdose, I had the very strong desire to make sure her death helped others. What I didn't know was how much my efforts for her death to help other people would help me.

That desire to give meaning to Chris's death led to the project with my son of interviewing people who had suffered losses similar to our own. It helped me so much to connect with people who had lost a loved one to addiction—I was helping them, and they were helping me. And, at the same time, Bill and I were grieving together—a win, win, win.

I remember interviewing a woman who had lost her daughter to an overdose. She told me through tears what a "sweet heart" her daughter had possessed. I identified with her description of her daughter's heart in my feelings about Chris, and I will never forget the rush of feelings her words stimulated in me. Our daughters had both been addicted to heroin and had died as a result of it. However, we both knew who our daughters had really been, despite their illnesses and the direction their lives had taken.

The same woman had also endured the suicide of her husband a week after her daughter's overdose. I was struck by her courage and ability to live on without both of them. She was a very spiritual woman who found comfort in her religion and prayer life. Although I couldn't relate to her spiritual beliefs, we connected in our stories and in the knowledge that our daughters were okay and we could survive without them.

I encourage you to find ways to share your experiences and to learn how to be present in a different way to the pain and sorrow of others. There is a tradition from the Native American culture called "Story Medicine," and I have found it is the best medicine one can imagine. It is the ancient tradition, which predates the written word, of telling each other our stories. Poet Maya Angelou wrote, "There is no greater agony than carrying around an untold story within yourself." The "medicine" is getting it out to a receptive audience.

Sharing your experiences can be a tricky balance if you've both had big losses. Take turns listening and expressing your stories. There can be a kind of magic that happens when painful stories are shared and the human connection of compassion is sparked. Telling your stories and possibly even crying together can be amazingly comforting to both the teller and the listener. Finding a deeper compassion in myself turned out to be one of the gifts I received from my ruthless grief.

Encourage Personal Expression

One of the most important aspects of supporting others in grieving is leaving room for them to express themselves in their own way. Do not impose your ways on others; let them explore their own creative processes, and leave room for them to be somewhat ruthless on their own behalf. Encourage them to do or express whatever is in their heart at the moment, while helping them to be on their own side about it. Part of your intention can be to have no judgments about anything others need to express. Let them speak about shame or guilt or regret, and then gently remind them of compassion for themselves. There is no wrong way to grieve, but please be aware of the warnings in Chapter 3 about the risks of medicating, comparing, or isolating.

Showing Up for Those in Loss

My first conscious experience with death happened when I was in second grade. A little girl from my neighborhood in Queens died suddenly of a burst appendix. She was from a large family, and news travelled around the neighborhood that the youngest girl had died. No one spoke about it in my home (my parents didn't deal well with death—my father's mother died when he was eleven years old, but he never grieved her). We had not been close to the girl's family, but not speaking about her death felt like a deafening silence. I avoided speaking to anyone in the girl's family and felt bad about that. I couldn't face them and felt awkward and out of place anywhere near them. Not only did I not know what to do or say, but I felt as if they had a contagious disease, which I didn't want to catch.

In hindsight, I realize that I had no preparation or maturity to show up for that family. I don't remember my parents doing anything either. No one told me about just "being there," but at the time I don't think I would have had the capacity to do it. Although

I think it is a common and very human mistake, I always felt bad about my behavior around that death and knew there was something wrong with my response.

I remember having a similar reaction in college when a girl in my class lost her parents in a fire. I just avoided her until enough time passed that I wouldn't have to mention it. Another time a new girlfriend in graduate school lost her mother to cancer, and I didn't go to the funeral because I was going camping. Those mistakes linger in my psyche and were not my best behaviors, nor who I am today.

Today I know about showing up for people in their loss, whether that is to make a call, send flowers, or simply write a note. You can even stop someone who is grieving when you pass him or her on the street and offer an invitation to get together for coffee, or offer a friendly word of comfort, something like, "I've been thinking about you and wish you well."

Showing up is important and can take whatever form you wish. It's not about what you say; it's just about being with someone in a compassionate and loving way. Don't be the one who avoids people in loss if you can possibly help it. Any gesture will do, but do something if you have any feelings about what happened to them.

Be Generous

Because I am a psychotherapist, clients have recounted their grieving experience to me years after their loss. These experiences are embedded in their psyches because they were turning points in their lives, and psychic wounds don't just go away if not confronted and shared. All the details need to be told and witnessed.

In addition to being witnessed, it is necessary for grieving people to feel loved and cared for. They probably feel quite alone and even abandoned by the person who died. That can translate into feeling abandoned by the people around them. Be curious, and be as generous as you can with time and energy. Know that you are dealing with someone who might be cracked open. Don't open up a big, personal conversation and then leave suddenly or in the middle of the talk. Plan to be generous with your time.

Remember my friend Anita, who said she would never forget the turkey that neighbors cooked and left for her family? She said she felt loved and cared for, even though she had no appetite. A caring gesture can change everything for the mourners.

My friend Sam told me about how he felt seeing neighbors, who had had a similar loss, walking up his driveway a few days after his brother had died suddenly in a car accident. When he saw them approach, he knew that here were people who could understand how he was feeling, and that it was the first time he felt any hope that he and his family could get through his brother's death—the other family was proof.

The Art of Presence

David Brooks wrote an op-ed for the *New York Times* titled "The Art of Presence."* It's specifically about a family who lost one grown daughter in a horseback riding accident and whose other daughter was seriously injured a few years later when hit by a car while riding a bicycle. Her face was disfigured and would never be the same. The mother wrote an article for Sojourners.net, which sparked David Brooks to write about the art of being present to someone who is in grief and loss.

He describes how showing up for a friend or family member in loss requires sensitivity and what he calls "the art of presence." The term speaks for itself, but I love that being present is described as an "art." That requires a creative way of listening and an immediacy that puts both people in the moment in a very real way.

The family Brooks wrote about "said they were awed after each

---

*www.nytimes.com/2014/01/21/opinion/brooks-the-art-of-presence.html?_r=0

of their tragedies by the number of people, many of whom had been mere acquaintances, who showed up and offered love" and support from all over the world. That was definitely my experience, and it helped enormously. Don't think you are too distant from someone to make some contact. Sometimes the surprising gesture from someone not that close is one that touches your heart. For example, a well known hair stylist who was a friend of my husband Bob came up to me shortly after Bob died and said he would like to give me a free haircut and styling. I was a little overwhelmed by his generosity, but I still go to his salon annually for the gift of my amazing beauty lift, and it means the world to me.

Judging Who Shows Up and Who Doesn't

I have heard people say, "You really know who your friends are when you see who shows up." I strongly disagree. The people who show up are the ones who are able to, and there is no predicting who those might be. Think of Blanche Dubois (*A Streetcar Named Desire*) and "the kindness of strangers." Give support when you can, make a generous gesture of any kind, and encourage the griever to focus on who is there rather than on who is not.

My friend Anita was unable to deal with Bob's impending death and didn't show up to say good-bye, even though she knew he was dying. She did not come for the funeral or even make much contact. She had experienced much traumatic loss in her own life, and she was unable to deal with more. It probably could have helped her, and we could have helped each other, but I accepted her inability to show up at the time. A year after Bob died, she was able to come to his memorial. I know being there meant a lot to her, and she was especially grateful that I didn't judge her for not being there earlier.

During the second year after Bob's death, Anita and I wound up spending a lot of time together. We became much closer friends through sharing our losses and our pain. We even took an annual vacation together to the Caribbean for several years after we recon-nected. I found her to be an extremely soulful and compassionate friend, even though her initial response had disappointed me. Stay as openhearted as you can, and encourage those you are helping to do the same.

If you are close to someone who is grieving, I suggest you help them keep from building resentments about who shows up and who doesn't. Focusing on who does show up is so much more enriching for all involved. This is one of the many ways you can provide a voice of compassion and reason in a possibly chaotic and emotion-ally irrational environment.

The Ministry of Presence

There seems to be no way to predict who would step up and provide "the ministry of presence," as Brooks calls it*, and who would not. It is not about who was closer or cared more, but just who is capa-ble and/or willing to be there with sensitivity and love, when it is needed. The right people will be there, and the ones who aren't are missing a chance for a meaningful interchange.

Physical Gestures

Feel free to bring food or flowers or to make physical gestures of care. The nonverbal expressions of love to those who are grieving are as healing as the verbal interchanges. You might notice that the sponges in their sink are grungy or that they're missing paper towels, and replacing those can feel overwhelming to those who are grieving. Little acts of kindness can go a long way to help grievers feel cared about. I remember feeling touched when someone I didn't know very well arrived at my house with a big case of soda,

---

*www.nytimes.com/2014/01/21/opinion/brooks-the-art-of-presence.html?_r=0

and even though it was something I don't drink, others did, and I felt loved.

Cards and notes can be very nourishing and helpful. I still remember some things that were on the cards people sent after Bob died. One said, "If you think of me, I am there. Where else would I be?" That felt so warm and spiritual at a time when I felt totally bereft and alone. I could also keep the note with me and refer to it when needed. Hallmark cards have bad press, but if you are someone to whom words don't come easily, go through the cards in a shop and pick one whose visual and words express your own feelings. Just be sure to do something if you are at all touched by this loss.

Allowing Space

Sometimes I think we tell ourselves that the mourner needs a lot of space as a way to avoid the deepest part of our own grief. Those who are grieving often need less space than you would think, especially early on. When they need to be alone, I suggest being in the next room and available to help. A loving, helpful presence in the house is invaluable at times of deep loss. When you cannot be there physically or the relationship doesn't warrant such closeness, clearly express that you will be on the other end of the phone and "on call" whenever needed. Even if you've offered that, still check in with a phone call: "Just calling to see how you are. I've been thinking about you and want to know how it's going. I've also been thinking about (your loved one who died) and . . ." Do not assume that those who are grieving will call you if they need you. They might not.

People who are grieving need to know they are not alone. At the same time, they are often raw in different ways and desire aloneness. Being sensitive to others' needs means picking up on cues that someone is receptive, at that moment, to our version of "helping." One hopes that grievers will signal their wants or needs to the people around them, but sometimes they are unable to. They may not be able to say, "This doesn't help me right now," so you will need to watch for cues. You might even teach them that phrase to use with you and others.

Attunement

Very closely allied with the art of presence and giving the griever space is the concept of attunement, a concept that has been discussed and written about of late, particularly in regard to parenting. It is now widely known how important it is for parents to be tuned in to their children, to who they are and what their particular needs are at any given moment. There's a joke about parents who are unable to tune in to their child because they are only concerned with their own needs: "I'm cold, so you need to put on a sweater." That is not attunement.

Attunement is an ideal quality for helping people grieve. Whether you think someone should be crying more or crying less is immaterial—let them be. I've mentioned my friend Jeanette, who left her voice mail with her husband's name on it for three years after he died. (She has recently changed it to just her name.) I'm sure her callers feel better about it now that her message reflects who is there and who is not. However, Jeanette left that message on her answering machine as long she needed. Don't oppose what others do in their grief unless it is dangerous in some way. For everything else, let them be. There is nothing helpful about being the "tone deaf" person who arranges a big dinner for the griever when that is the last thing he or she wants right now.

Don't Cry Harder than They Do

As a therapist in training many years ago, I remember learning a basic guideline for helping people get through their pain, and how to give them space to feel their feelings while honoring our own. It's about not taking too much space with someone and giving him or her lots of room.

Here's the background: As a psychotherapist, when I hear a painful story, of course there will be times when I am emotionally touched, and I might cry some. There are schools of therapy (based on the medical model) that highly discourage the therapist from showing any emotion at all. However, my training was not traditional and was based on a relational model, where the therapist is very real with her clients. The rule of thumb I learned about this was, "Don't cry harder than your client." This is somewhat tongue-in-cheek, but also has a lot of validity. This is also symbolic, in the sense that any of your own unresolved grief can interfere with making a space for the person in loss to honor and express his or her own feelings. I learned to hold myself back enough to give my clients room to have their own experience without imposing mine on them. If I tear up while sitting with a client, I just breathe through it, and I might or might not tell them what my feelings were about after his or her own feelings have been fully expressed.

I mentioned early on that the griever needs to be able to say, "That doesn't help me right now" when others launch into long stories about their own losses. Be attuned to your audience, keep a damper on your own self-absorption, and be available to mostly just listen.

No Hierarchy for Grief

I have noticed that a kind of hierarchy can develop in grievers that is completely not helpful; for example, "Oh, you lost a child, so your grief is much worse" may or may not be true, but it is definitely not what the griever (or anyone) needs to hear. Remember that there is no comparing pain, and any comparisons fall short of what loss is really about. I have done some of my deepest therapeutic work ever with people who have lost a beloved pet; there is no comparing pain.

Avoid comparisons. Don't say, "I understand what it's like to

217

lose a child. A little girl in my neighborhood died, and that was hard, too." Even if the comparison seems more germane, don't make it. Each trauma needs to be respected in its uniqueness. Every story can be heard attentively in its own right.

Anger

People who are grieving are frequently angry. Know that as you approach them, they may come back with irritation or opposition. Let them. There can be a lot of statements like, "You don't under-stand," or "You haven't experienced this." Let the griever vent, and then come back with curiosity. "You're right. Tell me what it's like," can be very supportive to someone who is grieving. Be available to his or her anger, and know that it is just a very powerful part of the grieving process.

Sometimes I will say to a grieving person, "This will change you, so let it. Show up consciously for what is happening, and you will be more whole when you are through it." Sometimes this makes people angry; let them be angry. The transformative aspect of grief is one of the basic messages of this book, and that message may or may not be appropriate to express to the griever at any given moment. Use your intuition, but don't be afraid to confront someone's anger if you wish to say something that may be giving the griever a gentle nudge in one direction or another. Using the phrase "Of course you're angry" can feel supportive to the person who hears it. When one feels anger while in grief, it often doesn't feel like part of the process, so being reminded that it is can be affirming and sometimes a great relief.

Saying the Right Thing

When you are helping someone in grief, you may be concerned about having the "right thing" to say. Mostly, you will need to give up that idea so you can feel comfortable around the person who is

218

grieving. However, I do have a few more suggestions. Many grievers think they are doing it wrong, so it can be important and helpful to reassure them; sometimes the most comforting thing a griever can hear is, "You are doing a wonderful job." Remember the story I told about crying on the phone with my friend Shirley, saying I thought I'd been doing so well? Shirley told me I was doing well right then, while I was crying my eyes out. That touched me deeply and changed my view of what "doing well" in grieving really meant.

Talking About the Deceased

When I lost Bob and Chris, hearing how important each of them had been to people and that they were loved and appreciated was very helpful to me. Many people told me how much Bob had helped them and how funny and enjoyable he was to be with. Chris had been missing in my life and the lives of those around me for so long that appreciating her life was more difficult. However, many people told me what a wonderful young woman she had been and what a creative, unique spirit she was. Hearing people around me commenting on what Bob and Chris had meant to them literally warmed my heart and helped me through my losses in major ways. I needed to know that people honored who they had been to them and that they were remembered with love.

Communication and Platitudes

As with most communication, "I statements" are suggested, as opposed to "you statements." Gentleness is also a key to saying something helpful to the griever. Statements like, "When my mother died, what helped me the most was . . ." can be useful and supportive. "You might want to consider inviting someone to help you with. . ." is often more appreciated and more effective than, "You know what I think you need to do is . . ."

Do not tell the griever, "You'll get over it." People who are grieving don't usually want to "get over it." They need to feel what they feel. It's also not a good idea to say, "You will never get over it." Getting "over it" is the wrong approach, whether you say they will or they won't. Getting through it is what everyone needs, but someone who is grieving may only be able to hear that at certain times. "I know you can get through this," might sound better, but you still may tap into their anger, which is fine. Sometimes I do say, "You won't always feel this way." I needed to know that when I was in my deepest grief, and sometimes hearing it had a good effect.

Be sure not to say, "It's all for the best." Unrooted optimism can be very irritating and unhelpful to someone in deep grief. It is even important to be aware when a spiritual or religious axiom is appropriate or when it is not. "They are in a better place" can be fine if those who are grieving are torturing themselves with images of their loved one suffering in the afterlife or with their own memories and images of how the person died. If they are just crying and needing to feel sad, some spiritual soothings can feel out of place.

Don't try to shut down the mourner's feelings. There is a fine line between protecting yourself from your own sadness or unresolved grief and helping the person in loss avoid unnecessary suffering. An example of this is someone who is haunted by the image of a fatal accident and seems to be tortured by the traumatic memories. This would be a time to be more soothing and to affirm to the griever that his or her loved one is safe or at peace and not suffering in that way right now. Sometimes I need to keep my soothing thoughts to myself (and actually soothe myself instead of others) when someone seems to need to shed tears. I think of the medical term "a productive cough," which means coughing is bringing up toxic material that needs to come out of the body. In grief, the term could be "a productive cry," which would be when the griever needs to get out the pain and even toxins from the grieving process.

Exercising Patience

I frequently use the word *mystery* when I'm helping others grieve. When and how people die is a complete mystery. We cannot make sense out of the inexplicable. Most of us need to try to figure it out for a while, until we surrender to the fact that there is no logical reasoning to it. Remember, the griever is on a journey toward acceptance, and sometimes that can be a long and rocky road. Be aware of your own impatience. If you're feeling impatient with someone else's process, talk more to a third party or yourself about it. Protect the griever from any impatience you might have with the way he or she is grieving; a grieving person has his or her own timing, feelings, concerns, unique needs, and ruthlessness or lack thereof.

David Brooks wrote,

> I'd say that what these experiences call for is a sort of passive activism. We have a tendency, especially in an achievement-oriented culture, to want to solve problems and repair brokenness—to propose, plan, fix, interpret, explain and solve. But what seems to be needed here is the art of presence—to perform tasks without trying to control or alter the elemental situation. Allow nature to take its course. Grant the sufferers the dignity of their own process. Let them define meaning. Sit simply through moments of pain and uncomfortable darkness. Be practical, mundane, simple, and direct.*

Moments of Joy

There are moments of joy in situations where you would never expect to find them. Let yourself have them, and help the grieving person enjoy them if at all possible. I would also suggest making yourself available for laughter when it comes. Happiness can defi-

*www.nytimes.com/2014/01/21/opinion/brooks-the-art-of-presence.html?_r=0

nitely be part of someone's grieving process and your interactions with him or her. Someone who is grieving may have spiritual experiences and amazing insights and awareness that turn into a quirky perspective that can seem comical. Awe can turn to joy and laughter in a flash. There is a place for gallows humor or silly interchanges if the time is right. I remind you of how my friend and I laughed at what Chris was wearing in the coffin and saying that she would not have been found dead in that. It was shocking, but riotously funny at the time.

In conclusion: My basic suggestion about helping others grieve is to *just do something*. Don't avoid the situation, and have the courage to show up on some level, no matter what. One of the basic messages of this book is that full-spectrum grieving can lead us into full-spectrum living. You can help someone get there by being open to his or her own process and by being sensitive to all the parts of his or her journey. Paradoxically, this attitude and help can lead you into the fullness of living in your own life and enrich your sense of living, of dying, and of everything beyond.

THINGS TO REMEMBER

- When you are grieving, reaching out to others who are grieving can help you, too.

- Make room for each other's feelings if you are both in loss.

- People who are grieving need to know they are not alone. Encourage them to reach out to you or others, and also check in with them often.

- Don't try to fix the other person or the situation. Don't try to understand it logically. Just being with the person who is grieving and being present are often the most important aspects of helping others grieve.

- The "Art of Presence" often requires few words and is something to practice with everyone in our lives.

- Be aware of any judgments of the grief process of others, and don't make them. Be as patient as you can be.

- Practical gestures can be as important as words and are often remembered.

- Let the griever know that he or she is not alone.

- Attunement is part of helping others grieve. Trust your own intuition about them and what they might need at any given moment.

- There is no comparing pain. Every loss has its own character, pace, and experience. Allow for it with others.

- Be available for anger if a grieving person expresses it in any form. Remind them that anger is part of grief.

- People grieving also need to know that the person who has died was appreciated and is remembered.

- Beware of ungrounded optimism and platitudes. Allow for sadness and tears.

- Be available for moments of joy, as well as gallows humor, at unexpected times.

- Give them this book.

Twelve Steps of Grieving

1. We admit we are powerless over our grief, and our lives can become unmanageable if we decide we are doing it wrong or don't give ourselves permission to do it our own way.

2. We come to believe we can be restored to emotional balance and spiritual peace, possibly to be more whole than before our loss.

3. We make a decision to turn each day over to the loving guidance of a Higher Power by giving ourselves permission to be alive.

4. We take a fearless inventory of our assets and liabilities, espccially as they relate to the person who has died.

5. We admit to a Higher Power, to ourselves, and to another human being the exact nature of our wrongs.

6. We allow for the process of change in our lives with humility and grace. We continue to reach out to others and to a Higher Power.

7. We pray for the obstacles to our healing, like survivor guilt, self-hatred, fear, and envy of others, to be lifted from us.

8. We make a list of regrets and the obstacles to our peace of mind that still linger.

9. We make amends for the harms we have done by changing negative behavior patterns, by valuing the people who are still with us, and by gratitude for our own lives every day.

10. We take inventory of our progress on a daily basis.

11. We seek contact with Spirit on a daily basis and trust the guidance we receive.

12. We make an effort to help others in their loss and practice these principles in all our affairs.

These are the Twelve Steps of Alcoholics Anonymous adapted for use in the grieving process. They may or may not be ruthless, but they demand honesty and courage. It is my suggestion that people who are grieving set up small groups to gather and help each other grieve, using the Twelve Steps of Grieving as their guide.

References

Introduction

Levine, Stephen. *Unattended Sorrow: Recovering from Loss and Reviving the Heart.* Emmaus, PA: Rodale, 2005, 27.

Chapter 1: Shock and Awe

Dead Man Walking. Screenplay by Tim Robbins; directed by Tim Robbins; Susan Sarandon, Sean Penn, and Robert Prosky. Los Angeles: Gramercy Pictures, 1995. Film.

Sartre, Jean-Paul. trans. Stuart Gilbert. *No Exit and Three Other Plays.* New York: Vintage, 1989.

Sogyal, Patrick Gaffney, and Andrew Harvey. *The Tibetan Book of Living and Dying.* San Francisco: Harper San Francisco, 1992.

Edwards, John (Host). *Crossing Over with John Edwards.* New York: Kaufman Astoria Studios, Sixth Avenue Productions, Glow in the Dark Productions, and Studios USA. TV Series, 1999–2004.

Didion, Joan. *The Year of Magical Thinking.* New York: Knopf, 2005.

Chapter 3: Warnings

Mellody, Pia, Andrea Wells Miller, and J. Keith Miller. *Facing Codependence: What It Is, Where It Comes from, How It Sabotages Our Lives.* New York: Harper & Row, 2003.

Chapter 4: Feeling Lost

Lewis, C. S. *A Grief Observed*. New York: Seabury Press, 1961.

Chapter 5: Blame and Healthy Anger

In the Bedroom. Written by Robert Festinger; directed by Todd Field; Tom Wilkinson, Sissy Spacek, and Nick Stahl. New York: Good Machine, Standard Film Co., Greene Street Films, 2001.

Chapter 6: Obsessions

Kübler-Ross, Elisabeth. *On Death and Dying: What the Dying Have to Teach Doctors, Nurses, Clergy, and Their Own Families*. New York: Touchstone/Simon & Schuster, 1997.

Handler, Jessica. *Braving the Fire: A Guide to Writing About Grief and Loss*. New York: St. Martin's Press/Griffin, 2013.

Chapter 8: Grieving the Unheroic Death

Ruiz, Don Miguel. *The Four Agreements: A Practical Guide to Personal Freedom*. San Rafael, CA: Amber-Allen, 1997.

Faulkner, Raymond O., Ogden Goelet, Eva Von Dassow, and James Wasserman. *The Egyptian Book of the Dead: The Book of Going Forth by Day: Being the Papyrus of Ani (Royal Scribe of the Divine Offerings)*. San Francisco: Chronicle, 1994.

McGovern, George S. *Terry: My Daughter's Life-and-Death Struggle with Alcoholism*. New York: Villard, 1996.

In the Bedroom. Written by Robert Festinger; directed by Todd Field; Tom Wilkinson, Sissy Spacek, and Nick Stahl. New York: Good Machine, Standard Film Co., Greene Street Films, 2001.

Chapter 9: Identity, Roles, and Grief

Yalom, Irvin D. *Love's Executioner*. London: Penguin, 2013.

Chapter 10: The Magic of Acceptance

Woodman, Marion. *Addiction to Perfection: The Still Unravished Bride: A Psychological Study (Studies in Jungian Psychology)*. Toronto: Inner City Books, 1982.

Brown, C. Brené. *The Gifts of Imperfection: Let Go of Who You Think You're Supposed to Be and Embrace Who You Are.* Center City, MN: Hazelden, 2010.

Chopra, Deepak. *The Seven Spiritual Laws of Success: A Practical Guide to the Fulfillment of Your Dreams.* San Rafael, CA: Amber-Allen, 1994.

Alexander, MD, Eben. *Proof of Heaven: A Neurosurgeon's Near-Death Experience and Journey into the Afterlife.* New York: Simon & Schuster, 2012.

Sebold, Alice. *The Lovely Bones.* New York: Little, Brown, 2002.

Breathnach, Sarah Ban. *Simple Abundance: A Daybook of Comfort and Joy.* New York: Warner Books, 1995.

Kübler-Ross, Elisabeth. *On Death and Dying: What the Dying Have to Teach Doctors, Nurses, Clergy, and Their Own Families.* New York: Touchstone/Simon & Schuster, 1997.

Wilder, Thornton. *Our Town.* New York: Harper, 1957. Play.

Chapter 11: All That's Left

Rowling, J. K. *Harry Potter and the Deathly Hallows* (Book 7). New York: Arthur A. Levine Books/Scholastic, 2009.

Chapter 12: Helping Others Grieve

Angelou, Maya. *I Know Why the Caged Bird Sings.* New York: Random House, 1970.

Brooks, David. "The Art of Presence." *New York Times,* Opinion. January 20, 2014, New York. http://www.nytimes.com/2014/01/21/opinion/brooks-the-art-of-presence.html?_r=0.

Williams, Tennessee. *A Streetcar Named Desire.* New York: New Directions, 1947.

About the Author

Susan Carroll Powers, Ph.D., is a clinical psychologist who has been in private practice for more than thirty-five years in New York City and the east end of Long Island. After receiving her doctorate from Fordham University in the Bronx, she studied Gestalt Synergy with Ilana Rubenfeld. Dr. Powers has led workshops for many years and specializes in grieving and recovery from codependency in her private practice and at Onsite in Tennessee and the Caron Foundation in Pennsylvania, two major codependency treatment centers. She has studied Psychodrama with Tian Dayton, Ph.D., and experiential therapy with Sharon Wegscheider-Cruse.